W9-CLG-448

Revised / Enlarged

Job Résumés

How to Write Them
How to Present Them
Preparing for Interviews

J. I. Biegeleisen

GROSSET & DUNLAP / PUBLISHERS / NEW YORK / A FILMWAYS COMPANY

Table of Contents

Résumé-Selector Index

ABOUT THIS BOOK

Probably no other phase of personnel guidance and job procurement techniques is quite as controversial as that which relates to job résumés. In the first place, some eminent authorities contend that résumés serve no purpose whatever; indeed, not infrequently, résumés hinder, rather than enhance, the applicant's chances for securing an interview. These authorities claim that a well-composed letter that singles out a few of the applicant's qualifications, enough to arouse the prospective employer's interest in meeting the applicant face to face, is far more effective than a formalized résumé that attempts to tell all.

Others, no less eminent in the field, call the résumé "the passport to a job interview." They have much evidence to back up that contention. All you have to do, they point out, is to glance through the want-ad section of any newspaper or recruitment literature and you'll see that, in most instances, a résumé is a standard prerequisite for a job interview—especially for better-paying positions.

Then, to add to the controversy, there are diametrically opposing points of view as to just what should be included in a résumé. Some personnel specialists I have interviewed in the preparation of this book have urged me to advise the readers *never* to include a Job Objective heading in a résumé. Why limit your scope? Others urge you *always* to state your job objective. How is the employer to know what position you are looking for, if you don't know, or if you won't state it in black and white? Some tell you always to include the Reason for Leaving entry to explain why

you want to switch jobs. Others say that you should never explain the reason for leaving in the résumé; this is best left for the interview. And so it goes—each opinion is presented as an inflexible dogma—with a convenient rationale to go with it.

There are a number of helpful books on résumé-writing. Certainly this is not the first one. But this book is unique in this respect: the sample résumés that comprise the major portion of this book present a great variety of different styles of résumé construction, offering the reader the widest choice possible. If you leaf through these samples you will note that some résumés include a definite Job Objective, others do not. Some give priority to Education; some sublimate that aspect and emphasize Work Experience. A few give Reasons for Leaving. Most do not. The sample résumés shown vary considerably not only in content but in format as well. They did not all emerge from one résumé-making machine —same headings, same format, same length.

The résumés in this book have been carefully selected and edited, not to expound one man's (the author's) fixed idea of how a résumé should be written and presented, but to reflect a wide cross section of opinion arrived at through a national survey. The examples shown are modifications (both in content and form) of actual résumés, presented in photographically reduced proportion, to fit the page-size of this book. The layout—that is, how the typewritten copy is arranged on a page—comprises an important factor in the preparation of a résumé. The

7

total effect of the format is achieved through the proper relationship of copy to surrounding space. To best see this relationship a gray tone was used on all résumé pages. This visual aid in showing résumés in facsimile form comprises an additional feature of the book and helps to differentiate it from similar publications.

In the final analysis, the personal résumé that you evolve should be distinctly your own—in format as well as in content. The intention of the author was to present a flexible guide to résumé construction, not a copy book. If this purpose is achieved, he will feel he has made a valuable contribution to the literature in the field.

Section **1**

WHAT PURPOSE DOES
A RÉSUMÉ SERVE?

For the best jobs today, a résumé is in most instances a prerequisite for a personal interview. Even if the particular job you are aiming for does not specifically call for a formal résumé, it's a good idea to get down on paper, briefly and succinctly, those aspects of your background that bear relevance to the job you seek. It's a good idea for many reasons. Here are some:

A résumé is helpful when you answer a want ad, either in writing or in person.

If the job applicant is to apply by mail, the employer generally expects a résumé, whether the ad specifically asks for it or not. There is a good reason for that. The position advertised—especially if it's an attractive one—may draw many responses. The average employer or personnel manager, or whoever it is that does the interviewing and hiring, has neither the time nor the patience to wade through stacks of letters replete with irrelevancies. Of prime importance is the applicant's specific qualifications. The employer is likely to favor the person who presents a fact sheet that is concise, to the point and in sequential order. That in effect describes what a résumé is—a presentation of pertinent facts that points up the applicant's fitness for the job on hand. For the employer, the résumé serves as a preliminary screening device in the selection of applicants to be interviewed. In the event the ad calls for the applicant to present himself in person, a well-organized résumé is still worth the trouble it takes to prepare it. A résumé serves as a crib sheet to jog your memory in the matter of dates, names and addresses of previous employers, schools attended, years of attendance, courses taken, and so on.

In case you are not hired on the spot (you can hardly expect that to happen on better jobs), you have a much better chance to be re-membered—and to be called back at a later time—if you leave a copy of your résumé with the interviewer. That is good advice even if you have gone through the routine of filling out the firm's employment application card. Often as not, the application does not provide sufficient space for supplementary information about yourself, which in your case may represent one of the highlights of your background. If you have a résumé on hand, your interviewer may either file it separately or attach it to your application. Either way you have improved your chances for getting the job.

A résumé serves as a functional "calling card" when you make the rounds of firms you would like to work for, who have not placed an ad.

It takes a lot of stamina, persistence, and shoe leather to make "cold" contacts—as salespeople call it. This course of action involves mapping out a route for making personal visits to a select number of firms you'd like to work for, in hopeful anticipation of getting an interview, with or without the formality of a previous appointment. Many sales are made that way; many good jobs are landed that way, too.

We are not here stressing the pros and cons of this course of action. What we are underscoring is this: a well-prepared résumé will be your best ally if you are venturesome enough to employ this direct approach to job procurement. If you do not get an interview or no present opening exists, you may leave a copy of your résumé for possible reference at a future time. In the event that you do get a personal interview, a résumé will help materially in the process of self-introduction. Modesty may inhibit you from talking about the honors you have won at school, citations you have received, sales records you have established. You'll be less reticent about making these known if you present the person who interviews you with a copy of your résumé, which makes note of these highlights of your background, among other qualifications and credentials. The contents of the résumé invariably determines the direction the personal interview takes—and the impression you make.

You will make use of a résumé when you apply to an employment or personnel agency.

If you apply to an agency to help you locate a semi-professional or professional position, such as chemical technician, sales manager, art director, engineer, programmer, or most of the better-paying jobs on a similar level, you can almost rest assured that you'll be asked to submit a résumé. This has become standard practice with a growing number of large agencies and indeed with most personnel departments of leading firms. The résumé is the fact sheet used to match staff needs of the employer with the qualifications of the job seeker.

Though a formal résumé is hardly ever a set requisite for the lower-paying jobs with minor responsibilities, most interviewers, consciously or not, are apt to be favorably disposed toward an applicant who has the foresight to come prepared with a résumé or well-organized fact sheet. The applicant benefits directly in another way by having on hand the needed facts to answer most of the important questions usually found on agency forms and application blanks.

A good résumé serves as the most effective mailing piece in a direct-mail job-search campaign.

Your sales pitch may include a personalized letter, a favorable clipping about yourself from a newspaper or trade publication, or even a reproduced sample of your work. It's the résumé, however, that often gets the most serious attention from prospective employers.

Whether you organize your direct-mail campaign yourself, or have an agency handle it for you, the résumé is the one indispensable item in your entire job-search campaign via the mail.

A résumé makes it easier for those who know you to recommend you to potential employers.

It's surprising how many choice jobs are landed through word-of-mouth recommendations and "leads" by neighbors, relatives, friends and associates. Statistically, nearly one out of every four men and women gainfully employed today—on all levels from the mailroom clerk to the high-ranking executive—has found employment not merely on merit, but through personal recommendation. But you can hardly expect people to recommend you with any degree of confidence, or to steer you to a position compatible with your background and abilities, unless you make your qualifications known to them. Unquestionably, one of the most direct ways of achieving this is to supply your sponsors with a copy of your résumé. They can help you better if they know you better and have a résumé to refer to, or pass on to others.

A résumé serves another purpose not directly associated with job procurement. When you sit down to compile data for a résumé, you are forced, as it were, to take stock of your career up to the present. The résumé is a ledger which must show realistically, factually, almost impersonally, what you have accomplished so far, and which way you are heading. It's good to do this once in a while even if you are not immediately concerned with the task of looking for a job.

The primary purpose of this book, however, is to show you how to go about preparing a résumé with a specific vocational objective in mind. The information, advice or instruction—call it what you will—between the covers of this book will help you construct a successful job résumé, *custom-made to your personal requirements*, yet widely acceptable by employment agencies and personnel departments of business and industry.

To help you in recalling and organizing pertinent data about two major aspects of your background, namely *Education* and *Work Experience*, you may find the forms on pages 25-26 helpful. Details as to these and various other aspects of your résumé will be discussed subsequently.

WHAT POINTS OF INFORMATION SHOULD A RÉSUMÉ INCLUDE?

Identification (who you are, where you can be reached)

Name: It's best to give your full name, spelling out the first, as well as the surname. Example: Robert Dunn, not R. Dunn. The use of an initial forces the employer to guess what the initial stands for and whether the applicant is male or female. The applicant's gender may be gleaned from the general context of the résumé, but why annoy the employer with guessing games?

Address: Give complete address with a minimum of abbreviations. When used for states, the post office recommends its official two-letter designations. And, always include your ZIP CODE.

Phone number: You may, if you wish, include two phone numbers—your home phone and your business phone, if you are presently employed. Hint: Before you give out your business number for personal reasons, clear it with your boss, especially if you hopefully expect a barrage of incoming calls from prospective employers. Your sudden popularity may prove a source of embarrassment to you and may even be the cause of losing your present job before you've had time to switch.

Objective

Experts in the field of personnel and employment differ strongly as to whether a definite Job Objective should be stated in a résumé. Some say a Job Objective (Position Desired, Employment Goal, or similar heading) seriously limits the scope of employment. "Why specify a position either by a title or phrase that may not exactly correspond to an existing vacancy?" they ask. "If you don't pin yourself down to a specific job title, you leave the door open to be considered for one or more alternate positions—perhaps as good if not better than the one you had in mind." Others contend that very few employers will want to take the trouble to analyze your résumé in the hope of guessing what position you are looking for. State the job you want and define it as clearly and concisely as possible.

Use your own best judgment as to which reasoning to follow. Should you be versatile enough to qualify with equal confidence in two or more fields not necessarily related, the best advice is: prepare a distinct and separate résumé, each with its own job objective, custom-made to accent those qualifications which match the job you seek.

Personnel agencies catering to top-level positions often omit the heading *Objective* on résumés designated for important clients.

If, for whatever reason that seems logical to you, you decide to include a Job Objective in your résumé, it is sometimes helpful to state it in the form of a thumbnail synopsis. Example: "Young man, college graduate, with two years of practical experience in publishing, doing paste-ups and mechanicals, seeks position with advertising agency to do layout and design. Special interest in packaging." This statement, which reads like a Situation Wanted ad, accomplishes several things: it helps to introduce the applicant; it focuses attention on salient qualifications that are developed in depth in the body of the résumé; it clearly indicates a vocational objective.

Education

Schools you have attended: It is customary to list these in *reverse* chronological order; *i.e.,* the last school attended listed first, and so on down the line. In each case, include name and location of school, dates of attendance, diploma or degree conferred.

If you have contributed appreciably to financing your education, it would not be amiss to make reference to this, as evidence of enterprise, initiative and self-determination to pay your own way. "Financed major portion of school expenses through personal earnings and savings" adds a positive note to the résumé of any young person about to enter the workaday world. If your college education was financed by winning a scholarship, this fact deserves mention under the general heading of Education.

Major courses and grades: You may make reference to, or actually list, major courses. Do so only if they bear a definite and important relationship to your present professional interests, or the job you seek. If your grades were exceptionally high, list them. If not, don't advertise the fact. In general, give more space to your school history if you are a recent graduate with little or no work experience. If you are a mature job seeker with a number of degrees to your credit or have completed your schooling a long time ago, it would serve very little purpose to allude to more than the last two or three schools attended. Don't give space to your elementary or junior high school record. Nobody cares. It's what you have done since that counts.

In professional fields, such as medicine, engineering, or chemistry, it is often helpful to list technical courses taken, to pinpoint the area of specialization.

Extracurricular activities: This, as a subheading under Education, may call attention to some of the extracurricular activities in which you participated, or excelled. Example: Vice president of the senior class, member of the publications committee, director of the art club, library aide. Did you excel in sports? This can be a point in your favor, as an indication of physical agility, team spirit, leadership potential.

If you have had an extensive extracurricular record, you can be selective, singling out those activities that relate to your professional goal and have a direct bearing on the job you are presently seeking. Naturally, the more mature you are and the more practical work experience you have, the less space you will devote to school-oriented activities.

Work Experience

This section includes the following information: name and location of each firm you worked for, dates of employment, what your responsibilities entailed and, where possible, how well you carried out these responsibilities. It is customary to list the work-experience record in reverse chronological order, starting with the current employer and going back.

In compiling such information and allocating space to this phase of your résumé, bear this in mind: your prospective employer wants to know your entire employment history, but he or she is particularly interested in your most recent job—one which presumably represents your highest level of achievement. Give this the most space.

Firms you worked for: List each firm, giving general location—city and state are sufficient. Don't waste space on street and zone number. The small companies you worked for may require identification as to the nature of their products and services, and perhaps a word or two to indicate position in the field. If you have worked for General Motors, IBM, or an organization of similar stature, you need not sing its praises. You may, however, want to specify the branch or division you worked for.

Dates of employment: Indicate the years in which you began and left each firm; for short duration jobs, include the months. Don't leave any "holes" in the chronology of employment. Any unexplained gap will easily be spotted as the employer scans the dates. A break in the continuity may be open to suspicion or, at least, to question.

Title and Responsibilities: For each job listed, indicate responsibilities as well as title. A title or payroll position such as Shop Foreman, Account Executive, or Art Director, while suggesting in a general way the function of the position, does not reveal the nature and extent of the responsibilities. The position of shop foreman, for example, may involve supervisory responsibilities for two or three persons, or for a work force of 150.

Describe briefly the major and related responsibilities for each job shown. In some cases it is desirable also to list skills and familiarity with specific equipment, processes and techniques.

Whenever possible give evidence of how well you carried out your responsibilities. Just to state you were eminently successful in all you have undertaken is at best a generality. What lends substance to claims are statistics. A sales manager's statement that he was "instrumental in increasing sales" is made more meaningful if it is backed up with figures showing percentage increase in volume of business or company profits, directly attributable to his efforts. It helps considerably to give a sampling of activities which brought about the results shown—developing new markets, setting up a sales-incentive program, liaison with production or research to improve quality of product while decreasing the production and distribution costs, and so on. If you have developed a new idea or system,

that's fine; but the more important thing is how it was beneficial to the company. Was it a success? Back up your claims!

If your work experience is diversified or has extended over a long span of years involving frequent job changes, it is sometimes advisable to categorize your employment record *functionally* rather than chronologically. A functional pattern features a range of abilities or areas of experience rather than a year-by-year summary of uninterrupted employment. In a functional résumé, names of employers and specific dates are of secondary importance and may in some instances be omitted in part, or entirely.

In organizing your résumé on a functional basis, list each area of experience under a separate heading. Include under each, your function, responsibilities, and proven accomplishments. For an example of a functional résumé, see page 86.

Generally speaking, the more prevalent type of résumé is one based on a chronological arrangement. Most of the résumés shown in this book are of this type.

Personal Data

This can be brief or expanded depending upon the type of job you are looking for, and the amount of space available. For instance, if you are aiming for a position as athletic coach, detailed physical specifications are relatively more significant than they are for a position as researcher or accountant.

Generally, *Personal Data* on the résumé includes the following: date of birth, height, weight, marital status, number of dependents, condition of health. Color of eyes and hair in most instances is irrelevant. What if your eyes are azure blue? Will that make you a better auditor? On the other hand, there are situations when selected details as to physical attributes can have vocational relevance. An applicant endowed with a beautiful head of hair aiming for a job in the promotion department of a hair lotion manufacturer might conceivably improve his or her chances for landing the job by alluding to this personal characteristic in the résumé.

The question of age may be of some concern to job seekers past fifty. Bland omission of age is not advisable, since the applicant's actual or approximate age can in most cases be determined through his employment history. It is now widely considered discriminatory practice for employers to use age as a determining factor in the hiring of personnel and this item is not permitted to appear on employment information intended for distribution by employment agencies.

Height is mentioned, and weight, too, but weight is perhaps a more significant item. Obesity may suggest glandular malfunctioning, lack of physical agility, and in some cases ungainly appearance. If you are of normal weight for your age and height, state it. If too thin or too heavy, omit this item with the hope that during the interview, your other fine personal and professional qualifications will more than make up for this physical shortcoming. Use your best judgment here, as you would in the case of a physical disability. Briefly state the condition of your health. If it's excellent, say so. You may even want to indicate the date of your last medical checkup.

Your marital status has some significant connotations. As far as the résumé goes, you are either single, married, or widowed. If you are divorced, you are, for all practical purposes, single. There may be some residual prejudice lingering in the mind of your potential employer in hiring a person whose marriage didn't work out, ending in divorce, annulment, or separation. There may even be the lurking, though unfounded, suspicion of a security risk in hiring someone with present or past domestic complications.

In the main, employers tend to favor an applicant who is married and has a family. Such a person somehow represents greater stability, one less likely to be a job hopper. If you have children, you may say how many, but need not go into particulars about their names and ages. For positions involving considerable travel, the single person may have the advantage.

Under the *Personal Data* heading you may also state whether you own or rent the home you live in, and if you own a car. If you are willing to relocate and/or travel, there is an advantage in pointing that out in your résumé.

Mention your hobbies if they bear a relation to the position you are seeking. For example, if you apply for a position as security guard in a bank or similar institution, mention of active interest in athletics is a point in your favor. If it's a journalist job you're after, photography as a hobby and avocation is worthy of mention, since photography and journalism—especially reportorial journalism—quite often go hand in hand.

Military History

If you have had a distinguished career in the armed services, it is important to give it space in the job résumé, especially if the job you are seeking bears some relationship to that experience. For example, if you served in the quartermaster division where you were responsible for purchases and inventory of military supplies, this information certainly would reflect in your favor as an applicant for a position where purchasing and inventory control constitute some of the main functions of the job.

Use discretion in the allotment of space on the job résumé for service in the armed forces. Ask yourself, "Will this information help me get the job I want?"

Affiliations

This heading may include membership in professional organizations, learned societies, and significant social and civic groups. For most jobs, it's wise to omit religious and strongly political affiliations since they may be contrary to the sentiments and commitments of your potential employer. An active and wide acquaintanceship is a particular asset for people in sales, real estate and insurance. An applicant with a large circle of acquaintances presumably has a broader field of operation. "Every friend is a potential customer."

References

Seasoned employers do not regard references on a résumé too seriously—at least, not until they are ready to hire you. The real interest in checking your character reference, as well as other credentials, will come after you have made a good impression in a personal interview. Under the heading of *References* it is sufficient to indicate that they are available and can be submitted upon request.

FORMAT AND PHYSICAL APPEARANCE OF JOB RÉSUMÉS

Length of Résumé

Limit your résumé to one or two pages. If it is at all possible condense the information to fit on one page without crowding. This advice is corroborated by most employment agents and personnel managers who receive hundreds of unsolicited résumés each week. Some go as far as to say, in no uncertain terms, that they won't read a résumé over one page in length; that their dormant files are full of three- and four-page dissertations representing the hopeful career aspirations of ingenuous applicants. A résumé, whether it be unsolicited or in response to a specific job vacancy, should be short in words, but not in facts.

There are singular exceptions to this call for brevity. A case in point is a résumé outlining the special qualifications and heavy professional background of top-level executives in the $30,000-and-up salary bracket. Often such résumés are brochure-length presentations prepared by personnel specialists as part of a "packaged" job-search campaign. Even in such instances, many experts feel that a well-organized one- or two-page résumé can be more effective in securing the attention of prospective employers than an overly long listing of alleged qualifications.

Kind and size of paper; typing

Don't deviate from the standard 8-1/2" x 11" size just to be different. A variation in size (either larger or smaller) can prove to be more annoying than distinctive. An odd size requires special handling since most filing systems are made for 8-1/2" x 11" paper. Unless you are in the creative arts or in promotion and want the résumé to serve as a sample of your professional talents, don't break step with tradition. Let the "pros" take the risk.

Use the best quality of paper you can get, preferably white. The difference in cost between a good quality and poor quality paper is negligible compared to what is at stake. "Good paper makes a good impression" is a slogan in the paper industry. It's true in more ways than one. A fine quality paper takes typing and printing better, and enhances the total effect of the résumé.

Unless you are an excellent typist, get your résumé typed professionally—preferably on an electric typewriter. A résumé showing uneven pressure of type, irregular alignment of characters, erasures and other evidence of human or mechanical struggle can hurt your chances for getting the job.

An extensive job-search campaign may require fifty or more duplicates of a master résumé and it is essential that the original from which all others are reproduced be literally and figuratively letter-perfect. The reproduction can only be as good as the original.

There are a number of ways to get multiple

copies, but rule out typewritten duplicates produced by carbon sheets. It is most unflattering to any employer's ego to be on the receiving end of a résumé produced in this manner. To some extent this also holds true for copies by mimeograph or spirit duplicator. Xerox and similar photocopying processes, as well as offset lithography (sometimes referred to as multilith) are recommended for quantity reproduction. Technically, these processes are capable of producing facsimiles that come closest in appearance to the master copy. For quantities fewer than ten or fifteen, photocopies are recommended. Prices vary from fifteen to twenty-five cents per copy, depending upon quantity. In most instances you can expect while-you-wait service. For larger quantities you will do better in price—and in quality, too—to have your résumé reproduced by offset lithography. There is a nominal charge for the plate and set up for printing; cost of the production is based on quantity. The larger the number of copies, the smaller the unit price. There is an additional charge for retyping your résumé on a professional typewriter by a skilled typist. This is an optional service.

Arrangement and page layout

You don't have to be an artist to arrange the wording in your résumé to be typographically effective. A résumé is essentially an outline. Keep it that way—simple, consistent and uncluttered.

A well-arranged résumé is easy to look at; it is easy to read. To achieve this, organize your wording into compact paragraphs or thought groups under main and secondary headings. To accent salient points of information, such as duties, job titles, names of schools and firms, you may want to use underscoring or capitalization. This also helps to add variety and typographic interest to a page of copy. Leave lots of white space. There is no fixed pattern or standard layout. Experiment, if you like, to introduce a note of individuality, but keep this within bounds.

We advised previously, *leave lots of white space*. That's easier said than done. The chances are good that your résumé will require three, four, or more complete revisions, both in wording and in arrangement, before you manage to fit all the information on one or two pages, without evidence of overcrowding. It's been said, "The white space on the paper makes the printed space easy to read." Even professional résumé writers revise copy and layout several times before they arrive at a good presentation—one that is chockfull of pertinent information, yet looks uncluttered and is easy to read. Compare the two résumés on pages 34 and 35 to see how appearance and readability are improved not only because of change in wording, but also because of the typographic arrangement.

THE LANGUAGE OF JOB RÉSUMÉS

Résumés are written in a language not unlike that used in classified ads or auditors' reports. The style is factual, concise and space-conserving. A résumé briefly and almost impersonally states who you are, what your qualifications are, and the kind of service you can render to an employer.

A résumé is a statement of facts, not opinions, generalizations or personal convictions, no matter how noble. "It has always been my fervent hope...," "In this industrial jungle of dog-eat-dog...," and other such strong personal or editorial comments have no place in a résumé.

Use active verbs, such as "organized," "increased," "administered," "designed," "directed," and "initiated." To make for easier reading, use short simple words: *"try"* for "endeavor"; *"varied"* for "multifarious"; *"get"* for "obtain"; and so forth.

In a résumé it is customary to limit the use

of first person singular (I, me, my, mine) not merely to conserve space, but also to be freer to mention accomplishments without giving the impression of boasting. For transmittal letters, letters of application and similar correspondence, in which a more personal approach is appropriate, there need not be any arbitrary restrictions in the use of personal pronouns.

General Phraseology

Here are some examples of expressions and phrases applicable to certain aspects of the résumé. You may find these helpful both in the choice of words as well as in content.

JOB OBJECTIVE

- Opportunity to utilize technical and supervisory experience in the field of _____.
- Offer _____ years of practical experience in _____, qualifying for a position as _____.
- A _____ position utilizing interest and training in the_____industry.
- _____ trainee leading to account executive position with progressive organization.
- Major interest in a position in _____ with opportunity for further specialization later.
- To be affiliated with a _____ company as _____where responsibility may lead to top management level.

Here in full is a somewhat different and more individual approach.

- A "Gal Friday" who operates equally as well every day of the week seeks challenging position in busy advertising office.

EDUCATIONAL BACKGROUND

- Graduated in upper_____ percent of class.
- Financed expenses with _____-year scholarship.
- _____percent expenses financed by personal earnings and past savings.
- On Dean's List during _____ years of college.
- Earned special commendation for highest achievement in _____.

(If you don't have any degrees or diplomas to indicate extensive formal education, you may wish to choose from the following examples.)

- Have taken courses in _____ at _____as part of self-improvement program.
- Have successfully completed company-sponsored training program in _____.
- Passed _____-year, college-level test while in service.
- Extensive home-study course in_____.
- Completed_____years technical training courses at _____.
- Following high school graduation, have taken variety of courses whenever time and employment permitted. These include: _____, _____, _____, _____.
- As a plan for continued study in the field of_____, have completed the following courses:_____, _____, _____.

WORK EXPERIENCE (showing evidence of growth or special achievement.)

- Promoted to _____position with enlarged responsibilities and _____ percent increase in salary.

- Within ___ years of employment with the company, was promoted to the following positions: _____ , _____ , each with a substantial increase in salary.
- As supervisor of the _____ department, initiated a new system of _____, which reduced yearly operating costs by ___ percent and increased profits by over $ _____.
- Started as _____ with a staff of ___. Within ___ years was promoted to position of _____ with a staff of ___, and salary increase of $ ___.
- In my capacity as _____, had direct supervision of ___ employees.
- Have working knowledge of operation and maintenance of the following equipment: _____, _____, _____, _____.
- Have the following secretarial skills:
typing: ___ words per minute.
stenography: ___ words per minute.
In addition, can operate the following office machines: _____, _____, _____, _____.
- Yearly income increased by $ ___ during period of employment.
- Started as _____, promoted to position of _____ within a period of ___ years.

Here is a sample of a statement, in full:

As Administrative Assistant to the Vice President, duties ranged from writing sales-promotion letters to creating, scheduling and administrating sales-incentive programs and contests. When the company decided to enter the supermarket field, was assigned to survey this field and upon my recommendations, our sales force was increased from 16 to 32 salesmen, and its entire method of distribution was altered. Today, all major supermarkets and chain stores throughout the country have the full line of our products on display. Company profits have risen more than 30 percent each consecutive year.

REASONS FOR LEAVING

- To accept better position offering greater opportunities.
- To be discussed at interview.
- Left to complete college education.
- Merger of departments.
- Work was seasonal. Wished to secure steady employment.
- Firm relocated to different part of country.
- Little opportunity for further advancement.
- Desire to expand experience beyond the scope of present position.
- Left on amicable terms. Have letter of reference and commendation.
- Was offered and accepted position which promised greater scope.

REFERENCES

- On request. Please do not contact present employer before interview.
- Portfolio of work available for review.
- References on hand, and available.
- A personal interview will provide the opportunity to review my portfolio and to explore my qualifications.
- Copies of transcript of record and letters of recommendation available.
- Inquiries as to personal qualities and work record may be addressed to:

PERSONAL INFORMATION

- Own home; late model car.
- Rent apartment; free to travel as required.

- Served in Peace Corps from _____ to _____ .
- Finances in good order. No debt encumbrances.
- Speak, read and write the following languages: _____ , _____ .
- Available for full- or part-time work.
- Presently employed. Available upon _____ days notice.
- Security Clearance; Top Secret.
- Active in local and national civic organizations as time permits.
- Within limitations of time, have been active in community and civic projects such as _____ , _____ , _____ .
- Member of the following professional associations: _____ , _____ , _____ .
- Excellent health, last medical checkup _____ .
- Varied outside interests include _____ , _____ , _____ .
- Well groomed, good personal appearance, friendly disposition.
- Willing to relocate.
- Job related hobbies: _____ , _____ , _____ .

SALARY

- Currently earning $_____ per year.
- Negotiable.
- Commensurate with opportunity offered.
- Salary range: $ _____ to $ _____ .
- Salary to be discussed during interview.
- Opportunity to learn, rather than starting salary, is of major importance.
- Salary on last job: $_____ .

MILITARY SERVICE

- Veteran, honorable discharge. Served from _____ to _____ .
- Saw service in _____ , _____ .

- Received special training in _____ .
- Separated from military service with rank of _____ .
- Honorary military citations include _____ .

LETTERS
Covering or Transmittal Letter

No résumé should be placed in an envelope and mailed off without a covering letter. If the résumé is in response to a specific job vacancy, the covering letter should refer to the vacancy, and call attention to the résumé, which shows how well your total qualifications match the requirements of the job. Or else the letter may single out one aspect of your general qualifications that you feel will be of special interest to your prospective employer—an aspect developed in greater detail in the résumé. Whenever feasible, personalize your correspondence by addressing the letter, as well as the envelope, to a particular individual, using his or her official title. You can check the spelling of the name and verify the title by phoning for this information. In the event you do not know the identity of the advertiser (as would be the case in answering a blind ad with a box number) begin your letter with either Gentlemen, Personnel Manager, Manager of Personnel Department, or some such salutation—never with "To whom it may concern."

A covering letter should be brief and businesslike, and yet it should introduce a personal touch to distinguish it from routine correspondence. It should introduce the applicant and arouse the interest of the employer sufficiently so that the applicant's résumé will be given due consideration, thus paving the way for an invitation for a personal interview.

For a sampling of covering letters, see pages 28, 29, and 30.

The "Broadcast" Letter

This type of direct-mail promotion, commonly referred to as a "broadcast" letter, has many exponents among personnel counselors who claim it to be an excellent way—some say that it is by far the best way—to solicit job interviews through the mail.

The broadcast letter is mailed without a résumé. It is a short one-page missal highlighting the applicant's qualifications, equated purely on proven achievements. These are expressed in simple terse sentences, wherever possible quoting facts, figures and percentages. The essential function of this type of correspondence is to arouse an interest in the applicant and cause the employer to want to know more through a personal interview. Whereas a formal résumé generally goes into details about the varied aspects of the applicant's total background, education, experience, personal data and so on, the broadcast letter does not. In a sense, the broadcast letter is a preliminary to a résumé; it is not a substitute for one. A formal résumé will still be needed later, either during the actual interview, or as a follow-up.

For a sample broadcast letter, see page 27.

QUESTIONS AND ANSWERS RELATING TO RÉSUMÉ PREPARATIONS

As a recent graduate, how can I list work experience when I haven't had any?

You may have had work experience without realizing it; you may have held a part-time or summer job, been in "business for yourself" running a paper route, cared for lawns in your neighborhood, or engaged in other self-employment chores. In addition, you may have acquired practical-work skills in your extracurricular activities at school—selling advertising space for the school publications, operating a mimeograph machine, typing term papers, or tutoring with or without payment. Tabulate your experience and work skills, list them and then select those that relate to the job you want. Give yourself credit for these work experiences in or out of school, though you may not have held down a regular nine-to-five job.

Again and again we are told that résumés should be brief—no more than one or two pages in length. Why this emphasis on brevity?

This call for brevity requires some qualification. In preparing a résumé for unsolicited distribution, it is no doubt best to get all your facts down on one page. The situation is somewhat different if you are preparing a résumé in answer to an advertised job vacancy and you have some basis for assuming that the employer is as anxious to find a qualified worker as you are to find a potential employer. As an occasional advertiser the employer is not inundated with résumés, as are employment agencies, and is therefore more apt to read your résumé with sustained interest, even if it is extensive—especially if you are a person with unique skills. Generally speaking, however, the more concise the résumé, the better.

Why is it so few job résumés include photographs of applicants?

For one thing, in many states it is considered discriminatory practice for employers or employment agencies to require job applicants to submit photographs. Then too, except in unusual cases, as for example in show business, where physical appearance is often of professional importance, photographs serve very little purpose. In fact, they are potentially harmful. Your prospective employer may not like the way you part your hair (he may have none to part) or may think your ears are too large or your lips too thin. He may have a natural antipathy, which even he does not recognize, for the type of person your photograph represents you to be. Photography as an art is highly advanced, but the average passport type of photo is often unflattering and does little to enhance the value of your résumé.

Is there a prescribed sequence for the various headings in a résumé?

No. The sequence is optional and will depend largely upon the qualifications you feature and the position you seek. If you are a recent graduate with only your good scholastic record to speak for you, you may want to give priority to your academic background by giving it top billing. The résumé of a mature sales manager, on the other hand, with many years of successful work experience will list the employment record first.

I have held five different jobs with as many companies in less than four years. Should my résumé indicate "reason for leaving" in each case?

No. It isn't necessary, or advisable, to state the reason for leaving each job, especially if you were dismissed. You can explain the circumstances verbally if the subject comes up during the course of the interview. At no time, however, either in writing or in person, should you indulge in recrimination about former employers.

A lengthy explanation about why you left each job not only takes up valuable space in a résumé, but tends to dramatize the number of jobs you've held and may identify you either as a chronic job hopper or an incompetent, malcontent employee.

A brief statement such as "left to widen scope of opportunities" or "accepted position with more responsibilities and higher salary" is quite appropriate. But don't overdo even that, if it creates an obvious pattern.

How can I make my résumé different from those customarily received by agencies and employers?

The best way to achieve this is to make your résumé neat, well organized and well reproduced. It will be different enough; so few fall into that category.

If you use "gimmicks" or typographic stunts, you risk the chance of failure, especially if you are an amateur. Professional artists and advertising specialists often resort to such tactics, and even they do not always succeed. Example: Enclosing an aspirin tablet with a phrase such as "Mr. Employer, do you have a sales promotion problem? Here's your remedy—*me!*" An example of another such gimmick is to singe the edges of the résumé and feature a headline, "This is the hottest news in the industry," with a brief text that shows the revolutionary nature of an idea the writer has developed in the merchandising field. Unless improvising advertising or promotion gimmicks is your professional forté, and is in fact the kind of job you are looking for, the best advice is, stay within the bounds of propriety and restraint.

For a rather safe departure from the normal presentation, you may want to experiment using a slightly off-white or tinted paper. The printed matter for legibility's sake should be black, regardless of color of paper.

Does the general appearance of a résumé make much difference as long as the facts are there?

It always makes a difference, but to a varying degree, depending upon the nature of the job you are looking for and how much the prospective employer needs your services. If you apply for a job as proof-reader or secretary and your résumé has a sprinkling of errors in spelling and grammar, the "facts" outlined in your résumé attesting to your proficiency are automatically discredited. In this and similar instances, your résumé is in effect a sample of your work. On the other hand, if your talents, services or skills are so exclusive that you have a minimum of competition in your field—and a job opening must be filled quickly—it will be the *contents*, rather than the appearance of your résumé which is of prime importance. Normally, the appearance of the résumé makes a first impression on the employer—even before getting down to the facts.

Be sure that your résumé is not only factually impressive but visually impressive as well.

Should the matter of salary be included in a job résumé?

Salary is an optional item on a résumé. However, there are strategic reasons for its usual omission. If you stipulate too high a salary, you may price yourself out of the picture; if too low, you undersell yourself. If you wish, you may resort to the expediency of stating that salary is negotiable, giving a general salary range, or of mentioning your present salary.

In most instances, the salary question is best deferred to the time of the interview. At that time you can size up the situation more realistically in terms of the firm's prevailing salary scale and the extent of your work responsibilities.

In the case of a physical disability, is it considered "withholding information" if you do not refer to it on the résumé?

The phrase "withholding information" seems to have legal connotations. You are not guilty of breaking a legal or even moral code if you omit mentioning a physical disability that may prejudice your chances for an interview. If, however, the nature of your disability is a serious one, and may cause you embarrassment and loss of confidence if it comes as a total surprise to your interviewer, then it's best to make mention of the disability with some factual assurance that it has not impeded you in the performance of duties in the past.

Is it necessary to get the approval of anyone you intend to list as a reference, even though you feel quite certain that you will be highly recommended.

Yes, by all means. Your reference will be able to anticipate an inquiry about you and be mentally prepared with a statement of considered opinions and facts. It's especially important, also, to let that person know how many such inquiries to expect. For instance, if Mr. John Smith is your reference on a résumé, distributed to hundreds of prospective employers, he may be justifiably annoyed at the number of inquiries that reach him by phone or mail. Unless he is apprised of the extent of your intended distribution, he may show his annoyance at the intrusion, either by ignoring all inquiries or perhaps giving an unfavorable report. Good advice is therefore to obtain permission of the people you list as references and to inform them of the nature of the position you are looking for and the number of inquiries they may expect. It's also a good idea to give them copies of your résumé. For all you know, they may turn out to be good sources of job leads, now or in the future.

What is the consensus regarding résumés written by hand?

Unless you are particularly and justifiably proud of your handwriting, and the nature of the job bears some relation to the quality of your script, current business practice calls for a typewritten résumé.

It may be a point of interest for you to know that a number of large corporations place great importance on handwriting as a revealing factor in personality analysis of job applicants. To the discerning eye of expert graphologists employed by these corporations, a person's handwriting may reveal not merely obvious characteristics related to emotional stability, but specific aptitudes, leadership qualities, general work habits—even physical appearance.

Since most employers have neither the inclination, time nor ability to analyze your handwriting, it's preferable, except in singular instances, to show the best of your personal qualities and other qualifications in type, not script.

Should my résumé omit the heading of Education in the absence of degrees or diplomas? Though I have taken a variety of courses throughout the years, my formal education has been limited.

It would be a serious omission to entirely bypass your educational background simply because you have no diplomas or degrees. Your résumé should make mention of specific training programs you have completed, schools you have attended, courses you have taken and other evidence of self-improvement. An effort in this direction often makes a favorable impression on a prospective employer. Make the most of it!

In this as well as other aspects of your job résumé, select the facts that put you in your best light. Accentuate the positive.

Is it necessary to mention hobbies in a résumé?

Only if space permits and if they relate to the field of vocational interest. If you apply for a position as a piano tuner, it would be pointless to mention the fact that you are an expert skindiver. If photography is your hobby and you are in the field of journalism, printing, or selling photography supplies, obviously your hobby strengthens and supplements your vocational interest. If you end up with extra space on the résumé, you may mention your hobbies, guided by the above advice.

Is there any advantage in getting professional help in preparing a résumé?

If by professional help you mean slight revision in the basic wording, and preparing a master typewritten copy for printing, the answer is yes. Most résumé printers, for a reasonable fee, will help you to that extent. But it isn't normally necessary to seek the services of personnel specialists. A résumé prepared by specialists not only may be expensive, but also tends to smack of super-professionalism, which may be out of keeping with the personality and background of the average job applicant.

The information as well as the wide variety of sample résumés shown in this book should serve as adequate guidelines for you to prepare your own résumé.

SUMMARY OF WORK EXPERIENCE

Date of employment: from _____ to _____

Name and address of company: _____

_____

Company's products or services consist of: _____

_____

Name and title of immediate supervisor: _____

My title or position with the company: _____

My primary responsibilities included: _____

_____

_____

My secondary responsibilities included: _____

_____

_____

Specific examples showing how effectively I fulfilled my responsibilities:

_____

_____

List of skills, processes, and techniques relating to responsibilities:

_____

_____

Name and title of person most likely to give me a good reference:

_____

Salary: when I began _____ when I left _____

Reason for leaving: _____

SUMMARY OF EDUCATIONAL BACKGROUND

Years of attendance: from _____ to _____

Name and location of school: _____
_____

Diploma or degree earned: _____

Major courses of study: _____
_____
_____
_____

Related courses of study: _____
_____
_____
_____

Position or standing in class: _____

Awards, citations, scholarships: _____
_____
_____

Extracurricular activities: _____
_____
_____

Name and title of persons most likely to give me good references:
_____
_____
_____

SUGGESTED FORM FOR COMPILING EDUCATION DATA

JOHN DOE ⋮ 000 CONVENT ROAD, SYOSSET, NEW YORK 11791   PHONE: (516) 900-0000

January 14, 1975

Mr. John Jones, President
Snyder Industries, Inc.
733 Third Avenue
New York, N.Y. 10017

Dear Mr. Jones:

In my four years as General Sales Manager of a leading construction distributor in upstate New York, I directed the sales and leasing policies of the company line of products--power equipment for heavy construction industries.

During that time:

- Annual billings in outright sales and term rentals increased from $3.5 million to $10.75 million.

- Profits rose five-fold, from $150,000 in 1970 to $760,000 for the fiscal year ending May, 1974.

- Number of accounts have increased more than 400%.

The success I've had here and elsewhere in 12 years of selling is not a coincidence, or attributable to luck or magic. My special education in Business Administration (Harvard grad.) has helped some; more important than that is a natural ability to analyze a production-selling situation, and come up with an innovative program that leaves competition way behind.

What I have done for others, I am confident I can do for you.

I would be glad to make myself available for a personal interview where we can discuss how I can serve your company.

Sincerely yours,

John Doe

000 Mount Royal Avenue
Philadelphia, Pa. 19112
January 5, 1976

Mr. John Jones, Personnel Manager
S & W Food Processors Company
1510 East Walnut Street
Philadelphia, Pa. 19102

Dear Mr. Jones:

In response to your ad in the January 4 issue of the Philadelphia
Inquirer, I am taking the liberty of forwarding a personal resume
touching upon certain aspects of my technical background which
should prove to be of special interest to you at this time. As
you will note, my entire technical training and work experience
in food processing run parallel to the demands of the position.

I am presently employed as Chemical Engineer with Royal Foods,
1420 Broad Street, Philadelphia, Pa. For reference you may contact my superior, Mr. Thomas Benson, whom I have apprised of my
intention to leave under the most amicable conditions.

I will be glad to make myself available for an interview at any
time to your convenience.

                              Sincerely yours,

                              John Doe

Telephone:
WA 0-0000

COVERING LETTER FOR RÉSUMÉ ENCLOSURE

000 North Boulevard
New York, N.Y. 10468
April 11, 1976

Mr. John Jones, President
Jones, Smith and Associates
1620 West Broadway
New York, N.Y. 10011

Dear Mr. Jones:

Your display ad in last Sunday's Times for an Art Director in
Cosmetic Package Design is of special interest to me because
it calls for qualifications which completely correspond to my
background and job objective.

You will note from my resume herewith enclosed that in addition
to an excellent professional background in general advertising
with emphasis on cosmetics, I have had particular success in
package design, having twice this year been awarded citations
by the Package Council for outstanding innovations in cosmetic
merchandising.

It is time for me to move on to a company such as yours, which
I consider to be one of the most progressive young packaging
design agencies in the field. I am young too, and at 27 have
had five years of hard core experience--and am ready for new
challenges which I know will await me as art director with your
firm.

May I ask you to read the resume and permit me to phone your
secretary next week for an appointment and showing of portfolio?
I look forward to meeting with you.

                              Sincerely yours,

                              John Doe

Telephone:
WA 0-0000

000 Blue Island Avenue
Chicago, Illinois 60607
July 10, 1976

Mr. John Jones, Personnel Manager
Barkeley Photos, Inc.
120 East Wacker Drive
Chicago, Illinois 60601

Dear Mr. Jones:

As a recent graduate, I understandably have not as yet had much opportunity to gain solid work experience other than part-time and summer employment listed on the resume, herewith enclosed. Incidentally, these after-school jobs not only furthered my interest and practical experience in photography, but helped materially in financing my college tuition.

Right through college, photography has been my professional goal (as some of the courses listed will show), with the hope some day to be affiliated with a progressive photo research laboratory such as yours. That day has now come.

I believe that my educational and technical background as well as my experience (limited though it may be) can be utilized by your firm to advantage, and look forward to an interview when I may have the opportunity to discuss with you employment possibilities. I have a portfolio of samples and the best of references.

May I phone you early next week for an appointment?

Sincerely yours,

John Doe

Home telephone:
(312) WA 0-000

PORTFOLIO OF
SAMPLE RÉSUMÉS

Note:
All résumés in this Section,
originally 8½" x 11", were
photographically reduced to
fit the page size of this book.

NAME
ADDRESS
PHONE NO.

. . . .

PERSONAL DATA:

Age ———— Height ———— Weight ———— Health ————

JOB OBJECTIVE:

Position desired: _____

Vocational goal: _____

EDUCATIONAL HIGHLIGHTS:

_____
_____
_____

PRIOR WORK EXPERIENCE:

_____
_____
_____

SPECIAL SKILLS AND ABILITIES:

_____
_____
_____

AVAILABILITY:

From week of: _____ Ending week of: _____

ADDITIONAL INFORMATION:

_____
_____
_____

REFERENCES: Personal and Business References available upon request.

JOB OBJECTIVE:

State type of job you would like with the company.
For example: A beginning job in _____
leading to a position in _____.

EDUCATION:

Name of schools and years attended, degrees you hold,
major subject field, special courses, awards and citations. (Space permitting, list courses which relate to
the job you are seeking.)

EXTRACURRICULAR ACTIVITIES OR OUTSIDE INTERESTS:

Select and list those school and club activities, hobbies or other outside interests which have a direct or
tangential bearing on your job objective.

EXPERIENCE:

List all part-time, summer, or volunteer jobs you have
held. Show how this work experience (limited though
it may be) has a valuable application to your present
job objective and future vocational goal.

Include useable work skills you have acquired, both in
and out of school: typing, operating business machines,
fluency in foreign languages, and so forth.

PERSONAL DATA:

Date of birth.......   Health...............
Height..............   Marital status.......
Weight..............

REFERENCES:

(This is an optional heading.) You may want to list
names and addresses of several people who know you well
enough to recommend you. In most instances, it is sufficient to say, "References Available."

PERSONAL RESUME

JOHN DOE / 000 West End Avenue, New York, N.Y. / WA 0-0000

OBJECTIVE: I am looking for a position where a person having multifarious background such as mine, can be given the opportunity to rise to the top by assuming
the duties and responsibilities in line with the conspectus of qualifications
outlined below.

EXPERIENCE: From 3/70 to present, serve as District Sales Manager for Ace Pharmaceuticals, located in Rayway, N.J. My responsibilities consist of directing
a sales force, selling and servicing accounts among druggists, hospitals, physicians, throughout the tri-state area. I am known to be very creative in my selling and am credited with opening many new accounts with sizeable increases in
sales. Assumed the position and responsibilities of District Sales Manager
after two years with a salary increase commensurate with superior efforts and
results. To spur on and upgrade our sales force, I have been instrumental in
getting the company to set up various in-service programs which were of great
help not only to our regular staff but to the additional personnel we hired to
augment our sales staff. In addition I saw to it that the quality of our products was improved resulting in great expansion of sales.

        From 1967 to 1970: Served as Display Supervisor with Adkay Displays
inc., located in Long Island City, New York. My duties and responsibilities consisted in planning and supervising window display installations in drugstores
throughout the greater metropolitan area, working with a team of installation
specialists. Having read about silk screen printing in a trade magazine, I
persuaded my company to open a silk screen department making it possible to re-
produce identical displays mechanically in any desired quantity. The firm's
business volume was $500,000 when I left the firm to take on another job.
From 1963 to 1967, served as Retail Chain Store Manager for one of the New York
stores owned and operated by the Robert Hall Company. Because of my obvious poten-
tials, was within three years made manager, although I started as a humble trainee.
Under my excellent supervision, our store received an award for the best decorated
branch of the entire chain. This came to the attention of the owner of a firm just
being organized to produce window displays for the drug and cosmetic fields, and I
was offered a job with a sizable increase in salary, to become the Display Manager
of the organization.

MY PERSONAL STATISTICS ARE AS FOLLOWS: I was born in Omaha, Nebraska in 3/3/41,
the third son of a business manager of a chain food store in that city. There I
attended Lexington Elementary School where I was graduated in 1955. When my mother
remarried, after my father's death in 1956, my family moved to New York City.
There I attended De Witt Clinton High School, Bronx, N.Y., graduating in 1959 with
a commercial diploma. After two years service in the Army, I continued my education
at Brooklyn Community College, Brooklyn, N.Y., where I was graduated with an Associate degree in Merchandising and Sales in 1963.
        Other personal statistics are: Height 6'2", weight 195 lbs., eyes hazel-
brown, hair prematurely gray. I am married, have two children: Johnny, age 10 and
Angelina, age 7½.
        I am an active member of: West Side Progressive Political Club, the local
P.T.A., Red Cross Community Drive, and a number of professional organizations.

EXAMPLE OF POORLY CONSTRUCTED RÉSUMÉ

(Compare it with the one shown on opposite page.)

JOHN DOE
000 West End Avenue
New York, N.Y. 10036
WA 0-0000

. . . .

OBJECTIVE: SALES EXECUTIVE for national manufacturer or distributor

EXPERIENCE: <u>District Sales Manager</u>, Ace Pharmaceuticals, Rahway, N.J.
Starting as Assistant District Manager, directed 12-man sales
force, selling and servicing accounts among druggists, hospitals, physicians throughout the tri-state area. Initiated
incentive plan resulting in 38 new accounts in highly competi-

1970
to
Present

tive market, increasing sales volume by 45% within two years.
In recognition, was promoted to District Sales Manager with
a $3,000 basic salary increase. Set up Dale Carnegie in-
service program, for continued upgrading of present force and
orientation for nine new salesmen added to the staff. Worked
closely with production department to improve quality of products, with expansion of sales volume by over 20% each consecutive year.

<u>Display Supervisor</u>, Adkay Displays Inc., Long Island City, N.Y.
Planned and supervised installation of drugstore displays
throughout greater New York area, heading 7-man team, doing

1967
to
1970

$250,000 volume of business. With company's approval, insti-
tuted silk screen facilities for printing identical displays
in large quantities. This resulted in firm's entry into the
syndicated display advertising field with a present sales
volume of $650,000 a year and covering New York and most New
England states.

<u>Retail Chain Store Manager</u>, Robert Hall Inc., New York, N.Y.
Began as Trainee to become Store Manager within three years,

1963
to
1967

being selected for this position over and above four others
with greater seniority. Worked closely with display dept.
in arranging interior and window displays, with our store
awarded "best display" citation for entire chain. Subsequent
publicity in <u>Display World</u> led to offer (at 35% salary increase) of challenging position as Display Supervisor with
newly organized firm specializing in window displays for the
drug and cosmetic fields.

EDUCATION: <u>Graduate, Brooklyn Community College</u>, Brooklyn, N.Y.
Associate Degree in Merchandising and Sales, 1963.

Professional training in Creative Selling Techniques and
Personality and Human Relations, Dale Carnegie Institute.

PERSONAL: Age 34, 6'2", 195 lbs., married, 2 children, excellent health.
U.S. Army, 1959-1961.
Member of Art Directors' Club, Sales Executive Club, American
Management Association, Vice President, P.T.A.

JOHN DOE
000 Marcy Place
Katonah, New York 10006
(111) 222-0000

Age 42 – Height 5'11" – Weight 165 lbs. – Married – Excellent physical condition

POSITION IN INDUSTRIAL RELATIONS FIELD UTILIZING
MILITARY EXPERIENCE AND EDUCATIONAL BACKGROUND.

EDUCATION:

B.S. degree, LeMoyne College, Syracuse, New York, June 1953
Major – Industrial Relations; Minor – Economics
3.43 (4-point scale) average; top 5% of class.

Honors: 4-year Academic Scholarship; Who's Who--
Dean's List; Industrial Relations Medal; Dorm Proctor.

Extracurricular Activities: Senior Senator in Student
Government; Class President, Junior Year; Student
Appeals Court Justice; Manager, Soccer Team.

MILITARY HISTORY:

Career Officer. Graduate, Air Force Officer Training School, 1954.
Served as manpower and organization consultant to top level management, Air Defense Command, Colorado; intermediate staff, 9th Aerospace Defense Division, Colorado; base operative level, Korat AB,
Thailand, SEA.

Service Experience Directly Related to Industrial Relations

-Conducted surveys on effective personnel utilization.
-Engaged in planning, establishing, streamlining phases of
 new aerospace programs.
-Effected savings of over $175,000 through a study of grade
 and skill requirements of missile unit of over 400 personnel.
 Received special letter of commendation.
-Planned organizational structures for all management levels.
-Headed a SEA manpower and organization team that provided
 managerial services to combative and supportive units,
 manned by over 5,000 personnel.

INTERESTS AND HOBBIES:

Extensive reading--mostly on Economics and American Labor Movement.
Swimming, Golf, Tennis, as time permits.

References Available

<pre>
                          JOHN DOE
                    000 West 181 Street
                    New York, N.Y. 10038
                         WA 0-0000
</pre>

OBJECTIVE: Part time, (after school hours and/or weekends) to work as copy boy or in similar capacity in newspaper office, hoping eventually to enter professional field in reportorial journalism.

EDUCATION: Presently in sophomore year at New York University. Major in journalism, minor in art. Secretary of Student Council; Member of Publications Committee and Student Art Staff.

Graduated Boy's High School, Brooklyn, N.Y., June 1973. 8th in class of 350; winner of creative writing medal.

Extracurricular activities included: active membership in Journalism Club, Photography Workshop, Spanish Club. Library aide for three years.

WORK SKILLS: Typing: 60 w.p.m. Office machine operation: Mimeograph, Rexograph, Ditto. Production: page layout, mechanicals, paste-up, scaling and retouching of photographs.

EMPLOYMENT: Summers, 1971, 1972: Newspaper route on commission basis. Summers, 1973, 1974: Caddy, Lido Golf Club, Westchester.

PERSONAL: Born: August 15, 1956 Height: 5'11"; Weight: 167 lbs.; Health: Excellent Hobbies: Photo buff. Do own developing and printing. Write short stories (unpublished).

Mother is author of series of children's books. Father, now deceased, was well known sports photographer.

REMARKS: Salary secondary in importance to opportunity to be and work in atmosphere of editorial department of large city newspaper.

REFERENCES: School and personal references when required.

JOHN DOE
000 Illinois Avenue
Norwalk, Conn. 07000
WA 0-0000

JOB OBJECTIVE:

To begin as MARKETING MANAGEMENT TRAINEE, with opportunity
to advance to account executive level.

EDUCATION:

B.S. degree, 1975; Cornell University, Ithaca, New York.
Major in Economics; minor in Psychology.
B+ average in both subject fields.

Tuition financed 60% through summer jobs; 40% through
Connecticut State Scholarship. Plan to continue graduate
work towards Master's degree in Marketing and Management
at the University of Connecticut, evening division.

Graduate, 1971; Central High School, Norwalk, Connecticut.
Business manager and chief ad solicitor for student
publications. Member of debating team, service squad,
student council. President of senior class.

WORK EXPERIENCE:

Production Assistant (Media Department) ---- Summer of 1974
    Harris-Gray Advertising Agency
Survey Interviewer ---------------------- Summer of 1973
    National Broadcasting Corp.
Assistant Bookkeeper -------------------- Summer of 1972
    French-American Banking Corp.
Door-to-door selling -------------------- Summer of 1971
    Encyclopaedia Britannica

PERSONAL INFORMATION:

Height: 5'10"   Date of Birth: May 1, 1953
Weight: 165 lbs.   Marital Status: Single
Health: Excellent

Enjoy reading. Follow stock market reports (a non-investor).
Chess, swimming, theater, as time permits.

```
┌─────────────────────────────┐
│         JANE DOE            │
│    000 East 74th Street     │
│    New York, N.Y. 10021     │
│         WA 0-0000           │
└─────────────────────────────┘
```

FORMER LEGAL SECRETARY, NOW 42-YEAR-OLD HOUSEWIFE
WITH TWO CHILDREN OFF AT COLLEGE, SEEKS POSITION AS
LIBRARY RESEARCH ASSISTANT IN COLLEGE OR PROFESSIONAL
LIBRARY, ON A PART-TIME BASIS.

EDUCATION:

Formal education included completion of two-year liberal arts program at
Endicott Junior College, Beverly, Massachusetts, graduating with Associate of Arts degree. This was followed up with office and secretarial
training at Gibbs Secretarial School in New York City.

WORK EXPERIENCE:

Prior to marriage in 1954, was employed in one-girl office of John Haberman,
a New York City patent attorney. In addition to general secretarial work--
typing, stenography, bookkeeping, correspondence--50% of my time was
taken up assisting my employer with research projects, including visits to
public as well as professional law libraries. It was this phase of my job
that I enjoyed best.

TIME AVAILABILITY:

Though my preference is for a ten-to-three work day, I will be glad to consider
flexibility in work schedule to suit time requirements of the job.

PERSONAL:

5'3"   –   126 lbs.   –   Excellent Health   –   20/20 vision

Am avid reader, enjoy outdoor sports and active participation in community
welfare organizations.

Husband is practising architect employed by Skidmore, Owings & Merrill,
New York.

REFERENCES AVAILABLE

Resume of ..... JANE DOE
000 Merrick Place
Garden City, N.Y. 11211
(516) 111-1111

POSITION DESIRED: EXECUTIVE SECRETARY and ADMINISTRATIVE ASSISTANT
                     for Major Law Firm.

EDUCATION: New York University, New York (1967-1968)
                     24 credits in business administration.

                     Pace College, New York (1966-1967)
                     Completed one-year program in Law of Contracts.

                     Andrew Jackson High School, New York (1962-1966)
                     Major in secretarial and business practice.

EMPLOYMENT: Legal Secretary and Administrative Assistant
                     Law offices of Ronald P. Murphy, Esq., 201 Main Street,
                     Valley Stream, N.Y. Specialist in Corporation Law.

1972 to date   Started as Legal Secretary. Within a year, was promoted
                     to Administrative Assistant in charge of office staff of
                     three, with salary increment of $1,000. Reason for
                     desiring change: Happy in my job, but would like to work
                     in mid-Manhattan, close to Hunter College, where I hope
                     to continue my education in the evening to complete credit
                     requirements for bachelor's degree.

1969 to 1972   Legal Secretary
                     Law offices of Harry Katzman, Esq., 500 Fifth Avenue,
                     New York. General law practice.

1968 to 1970   Legal Secretary
                     Law offices of Radner and Polokoff, Esqs., 666 Fifth
                     Avenue, New York. Attorneys for theatrical industry.

Summer, 1968   Secretarial Assistant
                     Law office of ex-Supreme Court Justice Sternberg,
                     185 Madison Avenue, New York.

PERSONAL: Age 25; Single; Attractive; Perfect health; 5'5", 115 lbs.

                     Enjoy swimming, ballet, reading, theatre.

SALARY RANGE: $10,000 to $12,000

REFERENCES: Present and former employers.

JANE DOE
000 Brookline Street
Hartford, Connecticut 00000
(111) 111-1111

TOP-NOTCH SECRETARY * BOOKKEEPER * TYPIST * RECEPTIONIST

seeks relocation in New York area to permit her to resume her education
at Pace College, New York City.

EXPERIENCE:

1974/date	J.P. Henley & Company Financial Underwriters Hartford, Conn.	Secretary to loan administrator. Handle cash disbursements, credit and processing of loans. Do reports and own correspond- ence from hastily dictated notes. Supervise 2 typists and 1 clerk.
1970/1973	Sterling Crafters, Inc. Custom-made Lampshades Hartford, Conn.	Secretary, receptionist, book- keeper. One gal office. Duties involved payroll for 18 employees, cash receipts. Assisted with advertising campaigns.
1968/1970	Clarion Enterprises Music Publishers Hartford, Conn.	In charge of accounts receivable, made bank deposits, used Friden Key-Punch, adding machine. Served as secretary to account executive, doing own and major portion of his correspondence.
1967/1968	"The Fashioneers, " Inc. Sportswear Designers Norwalk, Conn.	Office girl, typist, assistant bookkeeper. Occasionally served as model.

EDUCATION:

Graduate, Central High School, Norwalk, Conn. June 1967.
Senior Class Secretary; winner of typing medal.

Projected educational plans include evening study on college
level, toward degree in Business Administration.

PERSONAL:

Age 26; 5'4"; 121 lbs; excellent health.

JANE DOE
000 Riverside Drive
New York, N.Y. 10001
(212) WA 0-0000

....

OBJECTIVE:

To find employer in need of a Secretary whose ambition is to become Administrative Assistant.

**QUALIFICATIONS
AND
EXPERIENCE:**

Best expressed in the words of an ad my employer, Edward R. Smithline, placed in the classified section of Women's Wear Daily, upon my giving notice that I intend to resign as soon as he can find a replacement.

"I am losing my Best Girl. She types like a dream, takes dictation faster than I can talk, handles clients with tact and diplomacy, does library research, thinks, works under pressure, and SMILES."

My total work experience since finishing college has been with Sinclair Associates, 385 Madison Avenue, New York City--a fashion advertising agency employing 30 people. After 5 years, I plan to leave under most amicable conditions to diversify my experience in area of administration and management.

EDUCATION:

Pace College, New York, N.Y. 1968-1970
A.A. degree in Secretarial Studies.

High School of Art & Design, New York, N.Y. 1964-1968
Academic Diploma. Punctuality and Attendance Award.

PERSONAL:

Born August 11, 1950; Height 5'5"; Weight 122 lbs.
Appearance: well groomed; considered attractive.

AFFILIATIONS:

Assistant Secretary, Advertising Club of New York
Member, Advertising Women's Production Club
Member, Promotion Committee, local chapter, YWCA

REFERENCES:

My present employer:
Mr. Edward R. Smithline, President
Smithline Associates, 385 Madison Avenue, New York, N.Y.

Additional references available upon request.

JOHN DOE
000 Crotona Avenue
Sacramento, Calif. 90000
(213) WA 0-0000

OFFERING OVER 15 YEARS EXPERIENCE IN INDUSTRIAL MANAGEMENT
WITH RECORD FOR LOWERING PRODUCTION COSTS AND INCREASING COMPANY PROFITS

EXPERIENCE:

GENERAL MANAGER, reporting to President.
    The Wilson Corporation, Sacramento, Calif.
    (Food processors; sales volume $11 million.)

1969-Date

Started as Assistant Manager. Worked out a highly successful program of cost control. This resulted in a 38% savings in manufacturing costs, as well as in sales and operating over-head. Was moved up to position as General Manager with complete charge of all operations in 1971. Plant capacity has been doubled; 5 new branches opened; with company profits rising to an all-time high.

OFFICE MANAGER, reporting to General Manager.
    Johnson Drug Corporation, Sandusky, Ohio
    (Pharmaceutical specialties; sales volume $4 million.)

1966-1969

Started as bookkeeper and accountant in 1966. Because of success in instituting a 30% savings in branch office and warehouse overhead, was made Office Manager in 1968, from which position voluntarily resigned the following year to accept an attractive offer from The Wilson Corporation.

ASSISTANT WORKS MANAGER, reporting to Works Manager.
    Royal Corrugated Container Corp., Sandusky, Ohio.
    (Shipping cartons for the food packaging industry.)

1960-1966

Started as record clerk in Receiving Department; transferred to Planning Department in 1962. Six months later was placed in charge of all clerical work in the department. Suggested changes in routing which resulted in salvaging 15% of pro-duction waste of paper and board, with a saving of $45,000 annually. In 1965 was made Assistant to the Works Manager in charge of production. Preferring office management work as a career, resigned to accept position with the Johnson Drug Corporation.

EDUCATION:

Southern Louisiana College, Hammond, Louisiana
    B.A. in Business Administration, 1960.
Dale Carnegie Institute, Sandusky, Ohio
    15-week course in Dynamics of Human Relations, 1962.
International Correspondence School, Minneapolis, Minn.
    Certificate, correspondence course in Accounting, 1965.

PERSONAL:

Age 37; Height 5'10"; Weight 170 lbs.; Health excellent.
Married, 2 children; Wife, school teacher.
Hobbies are golf and fishing, as time permits.
Avid reader, mostly biographies and books on economics.

JOHN DOE
000 Mayfair Road
New York, N.Y.
WA 0-0000

OBJECTIVE: To be associated with a substantial organization, assuming
                  full responsibility in office management and accounting as
                  CONTROLLER, or equivalent post.

                              * * *

EXPERIENCE: PIONEER LAMPSHADES INC., New York, N.Y.
                  Manufacturers and dealers of custom-made lampshades.

Jan. 1972   Assistant Controller. Supervised staff of eight persons in
   to   accounting and non-accounting areas. Handled complete
Dec. 1975   set of books through general ledger. Accounting work was
                  done on N.C.R. 3300. Handled payroll of 275 union, non-
                  union, office and sales personnel.
                       Compiled data for salesmen's commission statements.
                  In charge of payroll audits, payroll tax forms, cash dis-
                  bursements, vacation schedules and work scheduling.

                  FRANKLIN-REISS MANUFACTURING CO., New York, N.Y.
                  Leading metal stamping firm for pocketbook industry.

Feb. 1969   Fulfillment Department Manager. Started in the accounting
   to   department handling Accounts Payable. Duties included
Jan. 1972   periodic auditing of billing and compiling supporting
                  information.
                       Before the first year was up, was promoted to position
                  as Manager of the Fulfillment Department, with complete
                  responsibility for its entire operation. Reorganized the de-
                  partment, affecting a reduction in the work staff from 8
                  people to 5, yet increasing the work output by nearly 50%.

                  NATIONAL CARD CORPORATION, New York, N.Y.
                  Greeting Card Specialists.

Oct. 1967   Full Charge Bookkeeper. Started as assistant bookkeeper
   to   handling payroll of 100 union and non-union personnel.
Feb. 1969   Prepared invoices for typing. Advanced to position of
                  Full Charge Bookkeeper, reporting to Treasurer. Handled
                  a complete set of books through general ledger; prepared
                  financial statements, supplementary records, and all tax
                  returns.

ROGER T. LYONS INC., New York, N.Y.
Stock Broker, Specialist firm.

Nov. 1966
to
Oct. 1967

Assistant Cashier. Started as clerk handling reports of purchases and sales, and orders to buy and sell stocks. Advanced to position of Assistant Cashier, posting information of daily stock transactions for the company's own trades.

SANDERS ASSOCIATES, New York, N.Y.
Stock Brokerage firm.

Aug. 1963
to
Dec. 1963

Odd Lot Clerk. While working for New York Stock Exchange as Page, approached by above firm to work in their order department; accepted position at a substantial increase in salary. Handled orders for purchases and sales of stock for all trades under 100 shares.

NEW YORK STOCK EXCHANGE, New York, N.Y.

Aug. 1962
to
Aug. 1963

Page. Worked on the trading floor of the Exchange, relaying messages to brokers. Read off stock quotations verbally, for odd lot brokers.

EDUCATION:

Attended Institute of Finance (Evening Division), 1965 to 1970. Took courses in accounting, business law, Federal taxation, economics and management.

Presently matriculated student at Pace College (Evening Division), working toward B.A. degree in Business Administration.

EARLY
BACKGROUND:

Attended elementary and senior high school in the Bronx. Played varsity basketball for 3 years in high school. Vice President of senior class. Active member of the "Y", Boy Scouts and Neighborhood Youth Organization.

PERSONAL
INFORMATION:

Age 30; 6'3"; 210 lbs.; Health excellent.
Married, 1 child; Wife, legal secretary.
Interests: camping, golf, home construction projects.
Served in U.S. Navy, 1964-1966.

JANE DOE
000 38th Street
Woodside, New York 00000
(212) WA 0-0000

CAREER OBJECTIVE

Executive Position in Personnel Management involving major
supervisory and administrative responsibilities.

SYNOPSIS

College graduate with degree in Personnel Management. Major
courses include: Personnel Interviewing, Industrial Psychology,
Psychological Testing, Human Relations, Management Training,
Labor Laws.

Diversified business experience in office procedures involving:
office supervision of personnel, liaison with executive staff,
preparation of reports and office memoranda, correspondence.

WORK EXPERIENCE

Metropolitan Container Corp., New York City

1970
to
Present

As Executive Secretary to the Sales Manager of the Corrugated
Container Division, have varied responsibilities ranging from
the customary secretarial duties, to charge of the Sales Manager's office in his absence, involving some independent decision authority.

Responsibilities encompass (in addition to the usual office
activities and procedures) decision authorization on matters
of price quotations, information on product line, customer
inquiries concerning shipment and special orders.

Deal directly with VIP's from parent and other companies,
handling travel and transportation arrangements, hotel reser-
vations, scheduling attendance at meetings.

Draft monthly reports on the division's sales volume for
presentation to audit department. Handle most of Sales
Manager's personal correspondence and records.

Credited with introducing a Dewey Decimal filing system
which proved to be so effective, that it was adopted by
other divisions of the company.

<u>Red Star Oil Company, Inc.</u>, New York City

1964
to
1970

As <u>Secretary</u> to the Manager of Technical Publications, had diversified duties beyond the usual secretarial responsibilities, including arranging of conferences, direct dealings with staff members on various levels, and editorial assignments.

Responsible for editing and proofreading of copy for technical publications, inter-office bulletins and newsletters, and arranging for printing and distribution.

Composed own correspondence to both domestic and foreign field representatives.

Directed the activities of two stenotypists assigned to our office.

EDUCATION

<u>New York University</u>, School of Commerce, 1969-1975
B.S. in Personnel Management, Jan. 1975 (evening session)

<u>Dale Carnegie Institute</u>, New York, Feb.-Apr. 1968
Effective Speaking and Human Relations

<u>Berkeley Business School</u>, New York, Feb.-Aug. 1964
Completed intensified secretarial course

<u>Central Commercial High School</u>, New York, 1960-1964
Graduated with honors, 10th in class of 340

PERSONAL DATA

Born: April 3, 1946   Health: Excellent
Height: 5'5"   Marital Status: Single
Weight: 119 lbs.   Finances: no debts, own car

Hobbies: Reading, crossword puzzles, swimming

REFERENCES

Excellent references available on request.

JOHN DOE
000 Delaware Avenue
Washington, D. C. 20000
(301) WA 0-0000

OBJECTIVE: INTERNATIONAL TRAFFIC MANAGER, with goal of becoming increasingly identified with international operations management; sales and marketing; planning, implementing methods and controls to develop and improve operations.

SUMMARY OF BACKGROUND: Sixteen years diversified and increasingly responsible traffic management experience. Have consistently demonstrated a practical yet imaginative approach to management responsibilities--always interested in seeking new ways to do things better, faster and more economically, and successful in building efficiency through the introduction of systems, methods and controls that get the desired results. Have been effective in supervising and coordinating personnel, maintaining esprit-de-corps.

EXPERIENCE:
1970-date

U.S. Government, Washington, D.C.
Traffic Management Specialist
...Establish regional operations for handling AID shipments to Africa and the Middle East. Currently engaged in the coordination of world-wide export shipments through contact with GSA regional offices, government agencies and transportation companies.

1964-1970

Smith Kline & French Laboratories, Philadelphia, Pa.
International Traffic Manager
...Managed an efficient traffic (export) department through improved business systems and effective use of personnel.

1962-1964

Pan American World Airways, San Juan, Puerto Rico
Assistant Station Cargo Manager
...Administration of office functions including handling of majority of correspondence and claims; supervised use of accounting procedures; worked closely with cargo manager on matters of policy.

1958-1962

United States Lines Co., Boston, Mass.
Freight Representative
...Held several positions with this firm. Began as assistant in export department...then in charge of steamship operations customs, purchasing, preparation of governmental statistical reports...promoted to position of Freight Representative in the Boston area.

(Please see page 2)

John Doe — 2 —

SUMMARY OF ACHIEVEMENTS:

Systems & Methods

Designed carbon inter-leaf forms using maximum amount of preprinted data; used master forms for replacing multi-sheet invoices as a time saver. After a six-month study (jointly with company's Systems and Procedures Department) a completely automatic invoicing system was designed to further increase the efficiency of the department.

Planning

Established priorities in clerical work with overall organization benefit in mind. Scheduled shipments to be consistent with personnel workloads. Assisted department head in making personnel forecasts, planning for average rather than peak loads. Assisted in planning layout of office of a department. Planned shipments to foreign plants, where timing and cost factors were most vital.

Analyzing Situations

Displayed in various ways an ability to analyze company departmental goals and to come up with a reliable solution. Solutions were both corrective and preventive as the problem presented itself. One corrective solution resulted in 30% increase in orders, introduced labor saving devices reducing shipping delays by over 50% in traffic department, and at the same time held down the requirements for personnel increases.

Personnel Handling

Supervised 30 people. Assumed responsibility of office management during transitory period between changes in managers. Reviewed applications and conducted interviews after screening of applicants by the personnel department. Assisted the department head at semi-annual reviews of job performance, and made recommendations for salary increases.

Liaison

Responsible for liaison between employer and outside associated organizations including sales representatives and others on sales-service administrative problems, invoices and payments; insurance companies relative to rates and service, and government agencies on details relating to licenses and shipments. Responsible for liaison-coordination with accounting department in regard to banking documents, systems and procedures, office layouts for department manpower.

EDUCATION:

Georgetown University, Washington, D.C.
B.F.S. degree (Shipping Major), June 1956.

Central High School, Charleston, West Virginia
Academic Diploma (with honors), June 1952.

PERSONAL DATA:

Age 38; Married, 1 child; 5'8"; 157 lbs.; Excellent health.

JOHN DOE
000 Kent Avenue
Trenton, N.J. 08000
(609) WA 0-0000

DIRECTOR OF PURCHASING

with top level experience in effective vendor relationships to buy at lowest cost without sacrifice in service or quality. Versatile background in interrelated fields in purchasing, accounting, and selling.

EXPERIENCE:

1969/date

PURCHASING MANAGER, stationery and printing; Milk and Cream Division, Sunshine Dairy Products, Hershey, Pa. Purchasing offices in Trenton, N.J.

The purchasing budget of my department runs in excess of $3 million annually. Of this approximately 25% is in office supplies and inter-office printing; 75% in dealer-aid promotion-- window and counter displays, posters, display stands, shelf talkers, etc.

-Because of thorough working knowledge of major printing processes (letterpress, offset, photogelatine and silk screen), am able to properly evaluate technical aspects of printed matter from the point of view of vendors' production costs and quality of finished product.
-Have stimulated vendor competition through fair and equal treatment to all with result that company prestige among suppliers and vendors is highest in company's 25-year history.
-Have initiated system of thorough investigation of vendors' position in the field, in terms of production facilities and management. Failures of vendors to make scheduled deliveries have been cut by 75%.
-Have instituted procedures for awarding orders based on sealed competitive bidding, resulting in savings of more than $200,000 annually.
-Attend production clinics, demonstration and trade shows to keep abreast with latest technical developments, to broaden scope of new supply and merchandising innovations. Subscribe to, and read major trade journals which have a bearing on purchasing, manufacture and line of company products.

1966/1969

ASSISTANT PURCHASING DIRECTOR, Ranther Company, Inc. Jersey City, N.J. Manufacturers of electronic units for the communications industry. Company employs 750 people.

    -Began as an Auditor, soon advanced to Junior Purchasing Agent, then to Assistant Purchasing Director; each step up accompanied by a 15% increase in salary.

    -Because of my 2-year army service with the Philadelphia Quartermaster Corps, was asked to handle government contracts for all phases of purchasing activities involving electronic components, machine parts, and test equipment.

    -Successfully expedited orders to maintain flow of material to meet rigid production schedules at costs below 20% of that of my predecessor, with highest quality of performance.

    -Gross income-profit ratio doubled during my 3 years with company. Letter of commendation by President of the company paid tribute to my ability. Bonus of $1,000 check accompanied the letter.

1963/1966

DISTRICT SALESMAN, Snow Crop Foods, Inc., New York.
Food Processors, employing 255 people.

    -Contacted chain and retail food outlets in central New Jersey. Promoted to chain contact man with responsibility to one of the large metropolitan New York chain organizations. Was top salesman among 18, with highest record of sales. Was selected to organize sales and distribution functions with three jobbers, increasing major outlets by 35%, with value of sales increase over 120%.

EDUCATION:

Rutgers University, New Brunswick, N.J. 1956-1960.
    B.S. degree. Major in Business Management.
Fairleigh Dickinson University, Rutherford, N.J.
    Graduate course in Sales Management.

PERSONAL:

Age 37; Height 5'11"; Weight 183 lbs.; Good health
Married, 2 children; U.S. Citizen
Own home and late-model car
Member, National Association of Purchasing Agents
U.S. Army; Quartermaster Sergeant 1960-1962

REFERENCES:

Business, Bank, and Personal References on request.

JOHN DOE
000 Saracen Street
Dayton, Ohio 44311
(513) WA 0-0000

PRINTING TECHNICIAN

GENERAL MANAGER, COMMERCIAL PRINTING PLANT;
CAPTIVE PRINTING AND/OR MAILING FACILITY

SUMMARY OF
EXPERIENCE

1971 - Date: MANAGER, PRODUCTION DEPARTMENT, with one of nation's most prestigious rate tariff bureaus.

Supervise staff of 23. Responsible for production of 50 million pages of tariff material each year plus all bulletins, dockets, miscellaneous forms and office copies. Mail 65 million pages per year to 9,500 subscribers who receive all possible combinations of 31 separate publications. Maintain mailing lists and subscription changes, new orders, inventories, warehouse operations.

Accomplishments: Affected annual savings in printing production costs in first 14 months on job; lowered production cost per page from .005 to .003; handled additional 1.8 million pages per month with a 36% savings over outside vendors' costs; increased production by over 60% without additions to staff; affected $1,200 monthly postage savings through installation of computer to sort address lists into zip code order for bulk rate mailing.

1970 - 1971: Ohio University, Athens, Ohio; Department of Office Services.

Involved in a one-year study of methods of operation in institutional captive printing plant. Published recommendations which formed the basis for reorganization of Addressograph Department.

1965 - 1970: HEAD, OFFSET DEPARTMENT; Reynolds Premium Printing Company, Akron, Ohio.

Initiated and organized new Offset Department. Complete departmental responsibility for production and sales; planning and directing work of 25 employees; preparation of printed items from copy to finished proof; estimating job costs.

1963 - 1965: SALES PROMOTION, SALES TRAINEE, Falco Paper Company, Sandusky, Ohio.

Served 3 house accounts. Technical trouble shooter on paper problems encountered by printers and lithographers.

TECHNICAL
SKILLS

WORKING KNOWLEDGE OF FOLLOWING:

Presses: Multilith 2024, 1850, 2550W, 1250, 1250W, MGD, Davidson 241, A.B. Dick 367, Kluge Letterpress.

Cameras: Itek 20-24, Ektalith, Xerox Model 50, stripping, opaquing, plate-making.

Bindery: Macey 12-station collator, Thomas Rotomatic collator, A & M rotary sorter, Baum folder, Rosback 6-station signature inserter, Rosback 3-station signature inserter with saddle stitcher, Myriad drill, Lawson drill, Challenge cutters.

Addressing: Addressograph 2600 Speedaumat with selector, Addressograph 1900 Record Card system with selector, maintenance of 70 lists comprising more than 200,000 coded plates.

EDUCATION
AND
TRAINING

Graduate, Central High School, Cleveland, Ohio.
Graduate, Printing Apprenticeship Program (typographers union) Completed 6-month evening course, company training program in Sales Promotion.

MEMBERSHIP

Production Men's Club; National Typographic Society; Advisory Committee, Vocational Training, Board of Education.

PERSONAL

Born.......... 5/1/42   Health........... Excellent
Height........... 5'8"   Married.......... 2 children
Weight .... 169 lbs.   Finances.......In good order

Outside interests - Technical literature. Collecting first editions. Fishing, golf and gardening as time permits.

REFERENCES AVAILABLE ON REQUEST

JOHN DOE
000 Loganville Road
Oakland, Calif. 91502
(213) WA 0-0000

. . . .

MARKETING-SALES MANAGEMENT

More than 10 years in marketing and sales management with
national and regional organizations, including new product
development, advertising and distribution. Experience
acquired while serving with:

<u>Fleming Drug Corp., Oakland, Calif.</u>
<u>National Foods Inc., St. Paul, Minn.</u>

OPERATIONS MANAGEMENT
1972-Present. As <u>Manager of Operations</u> with Fleming Drug Corp.,
Pharmaceutical Division, have supervisory authority for marketing,
production, distribution and accounting, with production facilities
located throughout the United States and Canada. Responsible for
the introduction and development of a computer program to provide
effective inventory controls. Achieved efficiency savings of more
than $130,000 during the first year of operation.

PRODUCT DEVELOPMENT
1970-1972. As <u>Product Manager</u> with Fleming Drug Corp., was
instrumental in initiating several new household products resulting
in highest margin of profits in company line. This was accomplished through coordination of research, production, highly effective promotional program and new packaging concepts.

MARKETING AND SALES
1968-1970. As <u>Regional Sales Manager</u> with Fleming Drug Corp.,
my territory comprised central U.S.A. (approximately 14 states).
Supervised a total of 53 brokers and salesmen. Affected 60% increase in sales through special marketing programs and developed
"spot" systems resulting in better customer distribution at lower
costs. Acknowledged as "The Regional Manager able to achieve
highest sales objectives with minimum expenditures."

1967-1968. As <u>District Manager</u> with Fleming Drug Corp., my
territory comprised five states. Increased sales 22% the first year
in a highly competitive market. Moved up to position as Regional
Sales Manager.

1964-1967. As <u>Wholesale Sales Representative</u> with National Foods Inc., early career experience was in selling to wholesalers and chain stores in a three-state area. Opened many new accounts which previous sales representatives had not been able to reach.

OTHER ACHIEVEMENTS

Consultant for major banking institution, analyzing marketing problems of small companies.
Inventor of closure devices and several product efficiency tools.
Feature writer for a number of trade journals including The Food Processor, Drug Trade Monthly, and Scientific American.
Recipient of Public Speaking Awards.

EDUCATION

Graduate, University of Wisconsin, B.S. degree, 1962.
Major in General Business, minor in Finance.

Special courses in Management and Computerization at:
Bradley University Graduate School; Louis A. Allen Management School; IBM School.

PERSONAL

Age 35, 5'11", 175 lbs. Good health. Married, three children.
Military background - Captain, U.S. Air Force, 1962-1964.
Secret clearance.

AFFILIATIONS

American Management Association
Board of Directors, YMCA
Sales Executive Club

Portfolio of records available

Synopsis of
RESUME
of
JOHN DOE

000 Wilmington Avenue
Lynchburg, Virginia
Phone: WA 0-0000
(area code 217)

JOB OBJECTIVE

Position in Marketing Management on Area or Regional Level
associated with the Electrical or Affiliated Industries relating
to Sales and/or Sales Engineering.

EMPLOYMENT

2/64-Present
General Electric Company
Communications Products Department
Lynchburg, Virginia
District Sales Manager

1960-2/64
Colorado Interstate Gas Company
Colorado Springs, Colorado
Communications Field Engineer

1957-1960
Communications Service Company
Hooker, Oklahoma
Owner and Operator

1954-1957
Peerless Oil and Gas Company
Hooker, Oklahoma
Drilling Superintendent

1952-1953
Varied jobs to support myself while attending school

EDUCATION

Formal:
Panhandle A & M College - 1952-1953 (2 years)
Basic science and math in preparation for
a degree in engineering. Left voluntarily
due to financial circumstances.
RCA Technical Training Program - Microwave
General Electric Sales Management
Psychological Aspects of Selling
International Correspondence School
Fundamentals of Electrical Engineering
Hold FCC Radio-Telephone License.

Service:
U.S. Navy - AEM/2c (1951-1952)
Electronics with a radar, radio-compass and
gyro-compass endorsement.

PERSONAL

Born: 2-2-33   Height: 5'11"   Weight: 190   Health: Excellent
Marital status: Married, 2 children   Finances: good order, own car

FOR AMPLIFICATION, SEE FOLLOWING PAGES
....

EMPLOYMENT HIGHLIGHTS

2/64-Present
GENERAL ELECTRIC COMPANY

    District Sales Manager for the states of Iowa and Nebraska. Sales responsibility of Company's products to Strategic Air Command, SAC Headquarters; State and local Governments; and commercial accounts such as Bell Telephone, American Telephone and Telegraph, Rath Packing Company, Wilson and Company, Iowa Power and Light Company; railroad, mining, trucking industries, and miscellaneous localized business.

    Hires, trains, and evaluates sales representatives. Makes territorial changes, prepares sales budgets and forecasts, investigates complaints, and makes recommendations for their settlement. Indirectly responsible for adequate service personnel.

    Originally hired by General Electric Company in 1964 as a Field Engineer. Due to proven success in helping to close some long-term pending orders, was promoted to District Sales Manager, Kansas City, Missouri. Transferred in 1966 to the Iowa-Nebraska District with a substantial increase in salary.

Results:

1) Obtained the first orders for the Company from the Kansas City Fire Department and the Kansas City Police Department.

2) Designed and supervised the building and installation of the first radio controlled Civil Defense siren warning system for Kansas City that later received national recognition and was written up by the Federal Civil Defense.

3) Designed and supervised the building and installation of a back-up communications system for SAC Atlas Missile Project.

4) Served in an advisory and consulting capacity on several occasions by request of the State of Nebraska.

Reason for Change:

    Growth in the mobile radio field has levelled with business depending more and more on the equipment change-out of existing systems. The severe shortage of frequencies available for new systems is limiting to a great degree future growth, expansion, and advancements. Desire to broaden experience and background.

1960-2/64
COLORADO INTERSTATE GAS COMPANY

    Employed by the Communications Department as a Field Engineer on new microwave system being built from Amarillo, Texas through Oklahoma, Kansas to Denver, Colorado. Upon completion of system, was transferred to Denver to help design an automated system of control for the City of Denver back to dispatch headquarters in Colorado Springs. This included telemetering, remote control of valves, and automatic control of compressor plants.

Reason for leaving: Colorado Interstate was denied expansion authority by the Federal Power Commission. Desiring to be associated with sales, accepted a generous offer from the General Electric Company.

1957-1960
COMMUNICATIONS SERVICE COMPANY

Successfully operated own business. Business built around the development of the Hugoton Natural Gas Field. Services performed included the design of communications systems, the service of these systems, and the erection and maintenance of radio towers. During this period, served as a consultant on communications to the Panhandle Oil and Gas Associations.

Reason for leaving: Drilling and development was near completion. Desired to enter into the new and fast developing field of privately owned microwave systems. Business was sold at a substantial profit.

1954-1957
PEERLESS OIL AND GAS COMPANY

Employed by Peerless to assist in the development of their subsidiary, the Plains Natural Gas Company. Performed a dual role as communications engineer; and, after a year of training, promoted to drilling superintendent with responsibility over three rotary drilling rigs and four strings of cable tool equipment. Responsible for the proper drilling mud consistency; the running, setting, and cementing of casing; the perforation, acidizing, and treatment and blowdown tests of the finished well. During the "off-drilling" season, responsible for giving welders tests and the supervision and inspection of pipeline contractors laying the gathering lines. During the last year of employment, company inspector while building multi-million dollar gasoline cracking and stripping plant.

Reason for leaving: Because of the scarcity of qualified and Federal licensed people to perform communications service, was approached by drilling contractors and pipeline contractors; and, with the sanction of Peerless, established Communications Service Company to serve all phases of the gas industry in that area.

REFERENCES

Available

JOHN DOE
000 Cordtlandt Street
Philadelphia, Pa. 00000
(000) WA 0-0000

<u>OBJECTIVE:</u>	Editorial position with large New York publishing firm, specializing in textbooks and programmed information.
<u>SUMMARY:</u>	More than 11 years experience as high school teacher and editor. Proven ability to work closely with authors: contract negotiations, guidance in manuscript preparation, production and promotion. Seek to relocate in New York area to expand professional horizons beyond present scope.
<u>EDITORIAL EXPERIENCE:</u> 1968-Date	<u>Managing Editor</u> of a small but highly prestigious Philadelphia book publisher. Work entails all phases of book production and supervision of a staff of three junior editors and two readers. Through personal contact with schools, and knowledge of curriculum structure, have initiated new department in programmed workbooks--a venture which has boosted gross annual sales by 35% on a profit margin considerably above the average return.
1964-1968	<u>Assistant Editor</u> with Hallmark Press, a limited editions publisher in Erie, Pa. Responsibilities included reading of authors' manuscripts, mark-up of copy, and proofreading. Liaison between editorial, art and production departments.
<u>TEACHING EXPERIENCE:</u> 1959-1964	Taught English and Social Studies in Philadelphia public school system. Special interest and training in course-of-study evaluation, visual aids, and curriculum construction. Faculty adviser, student publications.
<u>EDUCATION:</u>	<u>M.A. degree (Journalism)</u>, New York University, N.Y., 1957. B.S. degree, Temple University, Philadelphia, Pa., 1956.
<u>MILITARY:</u>	U.S. Army. Book reviewer, <u>Stars and Stripes</u>, 1957-1959. Honorable discharge with rank of 1st Lieutenant.
<u>AVOCATIONAL INTERESTS:</u>	Typophile (own and operate small hand press). Short story writing, painting, horseback riding.
<u>PERSONAL:</u>	Age 40; Married, 3 children; 5'11"; 162 lbs.; Health good.

JOHN DOE
000 Kennedy Drive
St. Louis, Mo. 90000
(000) WA 0-0000

Age 28 - Height 6'0" - Weight 160 lbs. - Single - Excellent physical condition

---

F R E E - L A N C E   W R I T E R

Special assignments for dynamic publishing company: field
interview research, non-fiction articles and books, including
photography when needed.

EDUCATIONAL
BACKGROUND:

M.A. in Journalism, Jan. 1973, University of Missouri.
    Named the outstanding student and most able writer among 400 at the
University of Missouri School of Journalism, in 1972. Earned 3.6 grade
average on 4.0 system. In top 5% of class. Major work in magazine-
feature writing and photography. Advanced graduate work in non-fiction
writing, feature stories, reporting, press photography, picture editing.
    Member, Sigma Delta Chi, national professional journalism society;
Kappa Tau Alpha, national scholastic honorary for journalism students.
Officer, Kappa Alpha Mu, national honorary photo-journalism fraternity;
Representative, Journalism Student's Association. Recipient of "Reader's
Digest" award for feature article writing.

B.S. degree, June 1968, Purdue University.
    Citation as Distinguished Student and Distinguished Military Gradu-
ate. Earned 5.0 on 6.0 grade system. Emphasis on accelerated writing
courses and economics.
    Member, Phi Eta Sigma scholastic honorary; Honor Key recipient
(four times); Dean's List. Served on campus magazine and ROTC publications staffs. Residence social chairman for four years. Campus
radio station announcer. College expenses financed through high school
savings and extensive part-time work.

WRITING &
EDITORIAL
EXPERIENCE

    Have written more than 150 full-length feature articles in addition
to numerous research and report assignments. More than 1,000 photos
in print. Have traveled some 30,000 miles in pursuing feature material.
Copies of articles in print now exceed 11 million. Article subjects range
from auto safety, business management, camping and economics through
retarded children, supermarkets, travel, used car buying and workshops.

    Reporter and feature writer on the "Columbia Missourian," daily-
Sunday paper for city of 50,000. Covered numerous feature assignments,
police and fire beats, hospitals, elections, accidents. More than 20
major features published in addition to six-day-a-week 'hard news'
pieces over several months. Many full page photo feature stories and
uncounted single photos.

Editor-in-Charge for "Chain Store Age Magazine," a 200-page monthly with 50,000 paid circulation. Interviewed corporate presidents, executives, financiers and managers. During initial six months with company, gathered information, took pictures for, and wrote more than 20 major articles, edited seven, and contributed to 15 other works for publication and publicity, with an aggregate total of 55 published pages. Also shot some 2,000 pictures, many in color.

Field Editor and Writer-Photographer for "Super Service Station Magazine," a 200-page trade monthly with an international circulation of 120,000. Left position for graduate work and advanced degree in journalism. Returned at full pay during 1974, covered 10 states and 5,000 miles by car. Gathered information, took pictures for, and wrote nearly 30 feature articles in 11 weeks. Continue to write for this magazine on a free-lance basis.

PERSONAL
BACKGROUND:

First of three sons of design engineer. Brought up in Chicago suburb of Park Ridge. Both parents Northwestern University graduates. Attended public schools, graduating from Maine Township High School (ranked among top 10 in nation). As honor student received special awards each year.

Commissioned Officer, U.S. Air Force, 1966-1968. In charge of writing and editorial-production work on base newspapers in three states. Received cash awards for management-efficiency suggestions. Was later promoted to office manager at S.A.C. headquarters, supervising eight men. Graduate of Air Force Effective Writing School. Honorably discharged as First Lieutenant.

PORTFOLIO OF CLIPS AVAILABLE

JOHN DOE
000 Pemberton Avenue
Boston, Mass. 00000
(000) WA 0-0000

· ·

CARDBOARD ENGINEER AND DESIGNER
with
million-dollar record of achievement offers his talents and services
to a young aggressive organization out to beat competition in the
corrugated display merchandising field by coming up with new ideas.

PROFESSIONAL BACKGROUND:

1967/Date - CHIEF DESIGNER, Display-O-Pack Company, Inc., an independently
operated subdivision of the General Paper Corp., a multi-divisional corrugated
manufacturer and converter.

Instrumental in organizing this division, I started with two assistants in 1967.
That year's business was $170,000. By 1969, staff increased to 6 designers
and model makers (whom I recruited and trained), and sales rose to $390,000.
At the present time, with no appreciable increase in staff, sales for this division have gone over the $1 million mark. Prestige of the company enhanced
through winning the Packaging Council Award, the Wolff Award, and the Point-
of-Purchase citation for creative floor stand designs. Customer list includes
Heinz, General Foods, The Borden Company, Colgate-Palmolive, Norcross
Greeting Cards.

Phenomenal growth of business and profits attributable to unique construction features built into design, several of which are patented under my
name. Floor stands are of one-piece construction, easy to pack and ship,
easy to assemble, and built to carry maximum merchandise weight.

My duties and professional experience extend beyond planning and
design. I confer regularly with sales managers, production department personnel, and directly with clients. I am thoroughly familiar with elements of
production--from the manufacture of the board, to printing (rubber plate en-
graving, offset and silk screen), die cutting, assembly, packing, shipping
and distribution.

1962/1967 - MODEL MAKER, Sterling Mounting and Finishing Co.,
Boston, Mass. Die cutters to the display field.

Work entailed planning and constructing dummies for folding cartons and
counter displays, marking out master sheets for diecutting, folding and
scoring. Organized schematic drawing brochure showing variety of display
units, tabulated by serial number for easy identification. Mailed as a promotion piece to all printers, lithographers, and silk screen processors in
the New England area, the response to this promotional brochure was far
more than anticipated--not merely in establishing good trade relations, but
in opening 15 new accounts with a corresponding 25% increase in business.

Additional publicity and business gained after parts of the brochure were reprinted (with permission) in Production Yearbook, Signs of the Times, Printing News, with a total circulation exceeding 50,000.

<u>1959/1962 – LETTERER AND DESIGNER</u>, Acme Display Co., New York. Industrial exhibit builders.

Work entailed creating visual concepts for industrial three-dimensional displays and point-of-purchase advertising material. Personal facility in typography, hand lettering, use of jig saw, cutawl machine, air brush was fully exploited to the advantage of firm, since I was able to "pinch hit" in any of these activities which did not require the employment of specialists on a steady basis. Through personal acquaintance with pro-motion managers of major firms, our company was given the opportunity to bid on over $350,000 worth of exhibit business, the major portion of which was awarded to us because of superior design and construction. Profits rose more than 30% annually.

<u>EDUCATIONAL BACKGROUND</u>:

    <u>New York University</u>, New York, N.Y.
        B.S. degree, 1959; Merchandising and Sales.
    <u>Parsons School of Design</u>, New York, N.Y.
        Two-year Associate Degree, 1957; Graphic Design.
        (transfer credits to New York University).
    <u>Brooklyn Technical High School</u>, Brooklyn, N.Y.
        Academic Diploma, 1955; Honor Student.

<u>AFFILIATIONS</u>:

    Member, Point-of-Purchase Institute
    Member, Art Directors Club of Boston

<u>PERSONAL DATA</u>:

    Age 37; Height 5'10"; Weight 180 lbs.; Health Excellent
    Married; Three children; Wife, art teacher

<u>PORTFOLIO OF WORK AVAILABLE FOR REVIEW</u>

JOHN DOE
000 Macomb Road
Larchmont, N.Y. 00000
(000) WA 0-0000

* *

DIRECTOR OF ADVERTISING AND MERCHANDISING

EXPERIENCE:

1965 – date   National Company with distribution in mass markets.
               (name withheld until job negotiations commence.)

PROMOTION MANAGER   (1971 to present)

Developed and executed a national promotion considered one of
the best in '74. Produced greatest in-store exposure in company's
history and achieved sales objective, 35% above estimate.

Produced and coordinated radio and outdoor campaigns, local
newspaper and TV spots.

Produced trade ad campaigns, direct mail, brochures, exhibits
and dealer aids.

Increased distributor-paid ads for product by 300% through
improved ad mat program.

Conceived a major industry-wide program, endorsed by all major
trade associations and written up in Sales and Merchandising
magazine.

MERCHANDISING SPECIALIST (1965 to 1971)

Developed and managed merchandising program considered one
of the most effective of its kind. Contributed to building company's stature especially in the supermarket industry.

Produced individualized promotions for chains in support of
packaged goods marketing. Sold 10 million promotion booklets
a year in which chains invested over $500,000. Program pro-
duced 140 million ad impressions a year for food and packaged
goods products on self-liquidating basis to company.

Assisted manufacturers and chains in solving marketing problems
in connection with major promotion projects.

Wrote and made presentations to agencies and manufacturers
resulting in 60% increase in business within two years.

Developed personal contacts with top management and operating executives of leading chain and wholesale organizations. Worked closely with trade associations. Represented company at conventions, at times participated on programs as speaker or panel member.

1962 - 1965   GENERAL MANAGER - Sterling Stores, New Haven, Conn.

Planned, opened and managed new branch store. Hired and trained all personnel. Met and surpassed sales objectives through outstanding personnel and community relations in highly competitive market.

1958 - 1962   BUYER, DEPARTMENT STORE - Simon's, New York.

Produced consistent profit in department with recent history of losses. Increased department's volume by 50% in three branches.

1956 - 1958   MERCHANDISING ASSISTANT - T & K Company, Inc., New York.

Sold to department and chain stores. Opened new accounts. Developed new items and merchandised new lines. Developed marketing plans for building a branded line.

EDUCATION:

1954 - 1956   Harvard Graduate School of Business Administration, M.B.A. degree.

1952 - 1954   Harvard College - social sciences, B.A. degree.

1950 - 1952   N.Y.U. School of Commerce - economics and statistics.

LANGUAGES: Speak, read and write German and French.

PERSONAL: Age, 43; Excellent health; Wife and three children; Own two cars; home.

JANE DOE
000 East 4th Street
New York, N.Y. 10000
(212) WA 0-0000

* *

PROFESSIONAL
BACKGROUND:
Diversified experience as staff art director, art editor, free-lance designer and illustrator, both in the United States and abroad.

(Abroad)

1961-1975

Art Director: Havas Conseil Publicite, Paris, France. Responsibilities included staff supervision and direction; purchasing outside art services for choice accounts such as Charles Jourdan Shoes, Evian Water, Cointreau Liqueur, De Beers Consolidated Mines, Sanforized Label, Moet and Chandon Champagne, L'Oreal.

Consultant: J. Walter Thompson, Buenos Aires, Argentina. Variety of special assignments in illustration, layout, photography, graphics, and promotional concepts.

(In the States)

1957-1961

Executive Art Director: Jamian Advertising, New York, N.Y. Layout design, supervising 3 assistants, client contact, selection and supervision of photography and type, idea formulation with copy staff.

Art Editor: Parents Institute, New York, N.Y. Credited with creating new magazine format "21." Worked with staff artists, editorial department, advertising department, with complete supervision of magazine, cover to cover.

Art Director: J. Walter Thompson, New York, N.Y. Advertising concepts, layout and illustration for choice accounts such as Cutex, Coty's, Pond's, Skol Suntan Lotion.

Assistant Art Director: Kenyon and Eckhardt, New York, N.Y.

Staff Artist: Batten, Barton, Durstine & Osborne, New York, N.Y.

EDUCATION
& TRAINING:
Academie de la Grande Chaumiere, Paris, France; 1966-1970
New School for Social Research, New York, N.Y.; 1956-1960
The Art Students League, New York, N.Y.; 1953-1956
The School of Industrial Art, New York, N.Y.; 1949-1953

PERSONAL:
Born 1936; Mother of 2 teenagers; Height 5'6"; Weight 126 lbs.

Desire to remain in my native country (U.S.A.) to give my family a feeling of permanence and stability, and take part in civic affairs and community life.

JOHN DOE
000 Barnes Avenue
Brooklyn, N.Y. 12100
(212) WA 0-0000

JOB OBJECTIVE:

Junior Programmer with major interest in data processing.

EDUCATION:

High School of Science, Bronx, New York; Graduate, 1968.
Drew University, Madison, N.J.; B.A. (math major), 1974.

College work included:

Analytic Geometry ------------------- 3 hrs.
Calculus -------------------------- 9 "
Advanced Calculus ------------------ 3 "
Differential Equations -------------- 3 "
Theory of Equations ---------------- 3 "
Functions of Complex Variables ------- 3 "
Theory of Probability --------------- 3 "
Methods of Mathematical Statistics --- 3 "
Linear Algebra --------------------- 3 "
Vector Analysis -------------------- 3 "
Programming for Digital Computers ----- 3 "
Physics --------------------------- 14 "

Technical training:
Electrical Computer Processing Institute, New York;
10-week course in Programming for IBM 370.

EMPLOYMENT:

Worked on various part-time and summer jobs to provide
100% of my college and technical training costs. Acquired skills in typing (65 w.p.m.), operation of IBM
Proof Machine, Monroe Calculator and other business
machines.

MILITARY:

U.S. Army, 1968-1970. Assigned to Armed Forces Special
Weapons Project at Sandia Base, New Mexico. Honorable
discharge. E-5 rating.

PERSONAL:

Born 1950 - 5'10" - 163 lbs. - Single - Willing to relocate.
Interests - Chess, model ship building, color photography.

References and other information supplied upon request.

JOHN DOE
000 Harrison Street
Honolulu, Hawaii
WA 0-0000

SYNOPSIS: Over seven years data processing experience as
             Programmer and Analyst utilizing IBM 360 (models
             30 and 40), IBM 370 (models 145 and 158), Basic
             Assembly Language (B.A.L.) and FORTRAN IV, mainly
             in the field of Antisubmarine Warfare (ASW).   Ex-
             perience includes large scale conversion from
             D.O.S. to O.S., feasibility studies, and system de-
             sign for RCA Spectra 70 and Honeywell 1250 and 2200
             computers.

EDUCATION   University of Hawaii - B.A. in Mathematics with
  AND   specialty in Business Data Processing and Accounting.
TRAINING: June, 1967.

             Technical Courses - A.N.S. COBOL, Basic Assembly
             Language (B.A.L.), FORTRAN IV, ALGOL, Data Communi-
             cations, Linear Programming and Operations Research.
             Graduated 1st in class.

EXPERIENCE: PROGRAMMER ANALYST   Sept. 1970 to Present.
             Staff of the Commander Antisubmarine Warfare Forces,
(full time) Pacific (COMASWFORPAC), Honolulu, Hawaii.
                Responsible for a major portion in the implemen-
             tation of the Fleet Antisubmarine Warfare Data Anal-
             ysis Program (FADAP), whose objective is to give Navy
             command elements from the Chief of Naval Operations
             down to the tactical commanders a means of evaluating
             ASW effectiveness data; design of forms and methods
             for immediate improvement in on-site collection, pro-
             cessing and dissemination of ASW data; design, pro-
             gramming and implementation of a system for computer
             editing, filing and retrieval of ASW data.
                Wrote programs for the RCA Spectra 70 computer
             in FORTRAN IV. Programmed the IBM 360 and 370 tape
             and disc systems in B.A.L.

             COMPUTER PROGRAMMER   Nov. 1969 to Sept. 1970
             U.S. Naval Examining Center, San Diego, Calif.
                Programmed on IBM 360 tape system to perform ex-
             tensive editing, scoring, and publish results of the
             semiannual Navy Advanced Examinations. Had produc-
             tion responsibility for a large scale EDP installation.
             Supervised 15 EDP operators.

COMPUTER OPERATOR   July 1967 to Nov. 1969.
U.S. Naval Station, North Island, San Diego, Calif.
    Operated and wired all IBM unit record equip-
ment and operated IBM 360 and RCA Spectra 70 computer.

EXPERIENCE: COMPUTER PROGRAMMER INSTRUCTOR   Feb. 1973 to Pres.
                 Honolulu Technical Institute, Honolulu, Hawaii.
(part time)   Duties include instructing a class of 26 stu-
                 dents in IBM 370 programming using B.A.L. tape and
                 disc. During the course of instruction added 200
                 hours of A.N.S. COBOL and FORTRAN IV. The students
                 write and debug programs on both the 370 and Spectra
                 70. In addition to instructing, am responsible for
                 interviewing, hiring and supervising all Data Pro-
                 cessing instructors.

                 COMPUTER PROGRAMMER   Jan. 1972 to July 1972.
                 Service Bureau Corp., Honolulu, Hawaii.
                     Wrote a complete system for the IBM 360 on con-
                 tract basis of 20 to 30 hours per week. System was
                 designed to expedite handling of hotel, airline and
                 tour reservations for groups ranging in size from
                 100 to 12,000.

                 COMPUTER OPERATOR   Jan. 1970 to Aug. 1970
                 ASC Tabulating Corp., Honolulu, Hawaii.
                     Worked 20 to 30 hours a week operating a Honeywell
                 2200 tape system.

PERSONAL: Age - 28   Married, 3 children   Secret Clearance

                 Salary negotiable; willing to relocate, government
                 will finance transportation costs.

                                REFERENCES ON REQUEST

JOHN DOE
000 Sommers Street
Washington, D.C. 20000
(000) WA 0-0000

COMPUTER ELECTRONIC ENGINEER

VERSATILE EXPERIENCE INCLUDES ELECTRONIC CIRCUIT DESIGN, RESEARCH AND PREP-
ARATION OF TECHNICAL PUBLICATIONS RELATING TO ANTISUBMARINE WEAPONS PROJECTS,
PREPARATION OF PROGRAMS UTILIZING AUTOCODER, IOCS FOR IBM 1440 COMPUTER.

EDUCATION: B.S. degree, Electronic Engineering and Mathematics, 1969.
University of Virginia, Charlottesville, Va.
Certificate, Engineering Administration, 1972.
George Washington University, Washington, D. C.
Certificate, Computer Programming Training Course, 1973.
International Tabulating Institute, Washington, D. C.

EXPERIENCE: PROJECT ENGINEER, Hanover Corp., Arlington, Va.
September 1971 to date.

Present work involves antisubmarine weapons equipment
research for NAVSEC, Department of Navy, and technical
writing on new Navy Underwater Swimmer Equipment.
Wrote technical manuals on TALOS booster handling band
locating fixture, revised Navy Technical Manual on hyper-
golic fluids, and worked on Marine Corps Technical Manual relating to mobile electric power supplies. Successfully designed and tested electrical circuit on prototype
of primate food dispenser for Holloman Air Force Base.

MILITARY: 2nd Lieutenant, U.S. Army Ordnance Corps, 1969-1971.
Branch and Automotive Maintenance Army Schools (5 months);
Maintenance Supervisor in repair of radio and signal equip-
ment and weapons, small arms (6 months); Supervisor of
Supply Activities (13 months).

PERSONAL:

Born	5/7/49	Health	Excellent
Height	5'11"	Marital Status	Single
Weight	171 lbs.	Finances	In good order

Willing to relocate; U.S. Citizen; Top Secret Clearance.

MEMBERSHIP: National Society of Professional Engineers
American Institute of Electronic Engineers

REFERENCES ON REQUEST

JOHN DOE
000 Leroy Street
Santa Clara, Calif. 90000
(213) WA 0-0000

SENIOR SCIENTIFIC SYSTEMS ANALYST

EDUCATION: B.S. degree, Mathematics and Physics, Auburn University, 1962.

Presently completing program of graduate study in Applied Mathematics at the University of Santa Clara, California. Courses include Applied Statistics, Applied Matrix Analysis, Advanced Numerical Analysis, Graduate Numerical Analysis, Programming, Graduate Programming, Complex Variables, Wave Propagation Theory, Quantum Mechanics.

EXPERIENCE: Barlow Aerospace Corp., Santa Clara, Calif.   1971 - 1974

SENIOR
SCIENTIFIC
SYSTEMS
SPECIALIST

-Responsible for data reduction and analysis of equipment damage studies. Using this information, planned new systems for data acquisition. Performed data reduction and analysis of part of Apollo system using multi-channel entry mode for information.
-Performed analytical testing of parts of system to be used in hardware selection. From data analysis, participated in the selection of hardware and system alignment.

National Computer Co., Santa Clara, Calif.   1967 - 1971

DATA ANALYST
SENIOR
APPLIED
PHYSICIST

-Participated in planning and selection of hardware to be used in diagnostic system. Work included supervision of control room, equipment, hardware, data acquisition and recording.
-Participated in the planning and specification of an on-line real time computer, to record and analyze large masses of information simultaneously.
-Planned and designed many of the diagnostic systems used in various tests. Recommended and purchased major portion of test equipment and systems needed for future tests.

Palmer Radiation Corp., Park Ridge, Ill.   1962 - 1967

DATA
ANALYST
JUNIOR
APPLIED
PHYSICIST

-Analyzed data from planned tests to see if systems performed according to theoretical determinations. Analyzed data from six different test systems and wrote up reports.
-Analyzed data from special 20 channel and 50 channel memory data acquisition system. Responsible for integration and reduction of special analysis data of bombs.
-Performed theoretical calculations of multibody scattering, to make it possible to use computers rather than operators, for applied analysis of photographic plates.

PERSONAL: Age 35; Married; Excellent health; Top Secret Clearance.

JOHN DOE
000 Overbrook Drive
Hartford, Conn. 00000
(000) WA 0-0000

ENGINEERING ADMINISTRATION

Associated since 1961 with civil engineering and construction firms in
progressively responsible administrative roles covering all operations
except technical. Possess practical working knowledge in civil engineering, but forte is in management, sales, coordination of multi-
project field activity operating controls, personnel, determination of
policies and effective procedural implementation. Highly successful
record in preparation and presentation of proposals and in maintenance
of client relations. No objection to traveling, relocating.

· ·

EXPERIENCE HIGHLIGHTS

──────────────────── 1970 to Present ────────────────────

Donnell Engineering Corporation, East Hartford, Conn.
Design engineers and supervisors of heavy civil engineering construction,
with permanent staff of up to 200.

Assistant to President

Responsibilities cover staff administration and coordination of new business
activities.

Have traveled throughout Central America and the Caribbean area on promotional missions, and maintain continuing new business through personal
travel and heavy correspondence.

Direct and conduct studies and projections to keep management informed
on status of projects, sales prospects, projected manpower, and income
figures.

Prepare and present proposals for new projects based on surveys.

──────────────────── 1966 to 1970 ────────────────────

Roberts, Kirschner & Stoloff, Indianapolis, Ind.
Civil and structural engineers with staff of 150.

Administrative Manager

First assignment with this firm was to open, staff and manage the Paris
office, to establish supervisory and inspection apparatus for $300 million
U.S. Military Air Base project.

ENGINEERING ADMINISTRATOR (page 1)

Selected and transported to Paris a group of 40 American Engineers, supported by 30 French technical and clerical personnel hired on the spot.

Appointed 3 key Regional Project Engineers responsible for the technical aspects of the work.

Handled personally, general administration, budgetary and other financial matters, and continuing negotiations with clients.

After this assignment (completed 3 months before schedule and 20% less than budget) returned to New York office.

Assisted senior partners in general reorganization of headquarters operations, formalizing policies and procedures in order to cope with rapidly expanding business. Served as coordinator (and frequent initiator) of comprehensive revisions of accounting, production and personnel.

———————————— 1961 to 1966 ————————————

Smithline, Robinson & Benton, Inc., Rahway, N.J.
General contractors, with permanent staff of 65.

Assistant to Vice President

Fulfilled from the beginning a varied assortment of administrative responsibilities issuing from the Vice President's office, primarily those concerned with customer relations and new business. Gradually assumed responsibility for all subcontract negotiations with building trades. Later appointed Project Manager to oversee 10 million dollar construction project.

PERSONAL INFORMATION

Associate degree, Civil Engineering Technology, 1959 – 1961.
Mercer County Community College, Trenton, N.J. (day session)

B.A. degree: Business Administration, 1964.
Columbia University, New York, N.Y. (evening division)

Age 34; Married, 3 children; 5'11"; 185 lbs.; Excellent health.

JOHN DOE
000 Bergen Street
New Orleans, La. 00000
(000) WA 0-0000

Born June 5, 1935
5'10" - 160 lbs.
Excellent health
Married (15 years)
Three children

```
┌──────────────┐
│              │
│              │
│    PHOTO     │
│              │
│              │
└──────────────┘
```

OBJECTIVE

To acquire a position as Company Sales Engineer, mechanical or construction related, with a sound company marketing a quality product.

FORMAL EDUCATION

M.B.A. degree, Harvard University, 1962. A- average.
B.S.M.E. degree, Ohio University, 1956. B+ average.
Heavy Equipment Sales Course, Carnegie Tech., July 1966.

MILITARY SERVICE

Captain, U.S. Army, 1956 to 1960.
Honorable discharge.

EMPLOYMENT HISTORY

Atlas Tractor Company   Sales Engineer
New Orleans, La.   June 1968 to Present

Effected sales of tractors and other heavy equipment to commercial and residential construction firms, logging operations, mining industries, farmsteads, and the United States Government. Clientele ranged from presidents of multi-million dollar corporations to pit foremen and farm bosses. Familiar with all types of construction and heavy equipment. Increased sales in my five state area 315% in seven years. Average annual income $25,000.

Blake-Hull Equipment Co.   Sales Representative
Baton Rouge, La.   July 1963 to June 1968

As Special Sales Representative of company was assigned to public relations and sales of heavy equipment to all open pit mining accounts for twenty western states. Increased sales 85% in five years. Average annual income $18,000.

GENERAL INFORMATION

* Will travel - will relocate
* Member, Nat'l. Society Mechanical Engineers
* Pilot's License, Single and Multi-engine
* Security Clearance - Top Secret
* Sports - golf, fishing and skiing

OBJECTIVE:

Position as TOOL AND DIE MAKING ENGINEER with major manufacturing company.

EMPLOYMENT
RECORD:

TOOL ENGINEER, in charge of machine shop of a leading manufacturer of printing equipment, located in Pittsburgh, Pennsylvania area.

1972-date

- Plan and design tools and special jigs needed for production and assembly.
- Consult with work supervisor in estimating time and cost of operational procedures.
- Periodically test machinery, replacing worn elements to minimize incident of breakdown during production time.
- Design many of the hand and machine tools which prior to my association with the firm had to be imported from Germany and Sweden at great expense and often with long delays.
- Developed system of multiple die stamping which lowered labor cost by over 45% and almost doubled production output of a major unit in a screen printing press.

FOREMAN'S ASSISTANT
Richter Die Works Inc., Milwaukee, Wisconsin.

1968-1972

- Started as Junior Die Maker and set-up man; within two years was promoted to Foreman's Assistant. In that capacity supervised crew of 8 (all with greater seniority) with excellent managerial-staff relationship. Was selected as trouble shooter, visiting customer plants to assure proper use of dies.

EDUCATIONAL
BACKGROUND:

Tool and Die Making Apprenticeship Program
    Mechanics Institute, Richmond, Va. Certificate, 1968.
Machine Shop and Industrial Arts major
    Central High School, Milwaukee, Wis. Diploma, 1963.
Home Study Gorrespondence Course
    Metallurgy and Heat Treatment Methods. Completed, 1971.

PERSONAL:

Age 30; Height 5'10"; Weight 180 lbs.; Married, 3 children.
Born in Dusseldorf, Germany; U.S. Citizen.

Military service, U.S. Army Engineer Corps.
Honorable discharge with rank of sergeant, 1965.

JOHN DOE
000 Decatur Street
Chicago, Illinois 00000
(000) WA 0-0000

....

SUMMARY OF EXPERIENCE:

Background encompasses eighteen years of diversified experience in the chemical industry in product management, technical sales, chemical processing, research and development. Have over three years of successful experience in selling to a variety of accounts--direct, through field outlets and brokers. Have sold to almost all levels of buying management. Have demonstrated unerring ability to forecast new buying trends, and develop new products for which there is a strong potential market.

PRODUCT EXPERIENCE:

Hydrolyzed Vegetable Proteins, Attractants, Lecithin, Soy Flour Coatings - alkyds, epoxies, polyurethanes, butyl rubber, acrylic, silicone, vinyl, polysulfide and polyester resins.
Plastisols
Adhesives - structural and non-structural
Inks and solvents
Detergents, dry starch and grocery products

BUSINESS EXPERIENCE:

ARLINGTON MANUFACTURING COMPANY, Chicago, Illinois
Product Manager - Sales and Marketing

1968-Present

In my official capacity, am responsible for national territory and export items, and accountable for achieving maximum profitable sales of assigned products. Work includes planning, executing and controlling approved market programs, as well as product specifications, advertising, research and technical service, sales guidance to 24 regional and district managers. In the past three years have guided the net profit to a 350% increase on increased tonnage of 100%.

Presently on special experimental project in Chemical Engineering Department involving chemical process work.

1965-1968

BAYLEY MILLS INC. - Chemical Division, Chicago, Illinois
Senior Development Chemist in Technical Service

Major responsibility consisted of providing technical assistance to customers, field salesmen, and production personnel. Organized technical in-service training program for sales force. Produced a 20-minute instructional film which has become an integral part of this program.

. . . .

1964-1965	SUPERIOR PAINT AND VARNISH COMPANY, Quincy, Illinois Technical Director

Responsible for development of epoxies, polyurethanes, iso-phthalic alkyds, and butyl rubber for finishes. Directed research and development of a new line of adhesives, plastisols and specialty compounds. The patented plastisol specifically developed for the automobile industry proved its superiority over competitive products. In the first six months, sales amounted to $250,000 and more than doubled at the end of the year.

1957-1964	PEORIA CHEMICAL COMPANY, Peoria, Illinois Product Development Engineer - Coating Section

Concerned with application of silicone resins in coatings, as well as providing technical service to customers and field sales force. Recruited, trained and supervised new sales and laboratory personnel.

EDUCATION:

University of Cincinnati, Cincinnati, Ohio
B.S. in Chemical Engineering, 1957. Honor graduate.

Bradley University, Peoria, Illinois
Certificate, 6-month course in Advanced Paint Technology.

MEMBERSHIPS:

American Society of Chemical Engineers
American Chemical Society
National Association of the Paint and Chemical Industry

PERSONAL:

Age: 40 .... Height: 5'11" .... Weight: 180 lbs.
Married .... 4 Children; Wife former school teacher
Finances ...... In good order, no debt encumbrances
Own home ..... Late and older model cars
Health........ Excellent; last medical checkup Sept. 1974

REFERENCES:

Personal and business references available on request.

JOHN DOE
000 Conway Street
Akron, Ohio 00000
(000) WA 0-0000

<u>WELDING TECHNOLOGY ENGINEER</u>

WITH OVER 12 YEARS OF HARD CORE LABORATORY AND PRODUCTION EXPERIENCE

EXPERIENCE:

1971/date

<u>SENIOR ENGINEER</u> with one of country's leading producers of instantaneous facsimile duplicating devices, and pioneers in photocopying field. My responsibilities encompass:

<u>Value Analysis</u>: As team leader supervising staff of 28 engineers and production specialists, am in charge of evaluating reliability and cost factors of new production machines. Assignment in all phases of research and manufacturing, plus tooling and assembly production cost accounting, and inventory control. Based on last year's schedules, product savings amounted to $750,000.

<u>Advanced Fabrication Technology</u>: Work with design and research engineers in determining feasibility of new machines and equipment, devising testing procedures for efficiency in production and service. Consult with vendors on prototype construction of machine parts.

<u>Process Development</u>: Review new manufacturing techniques prior to establishing technical and economic feasibility. Recommend changes when necessary.

1968/1971

<u>LABORATORY ENGINEER</u>, Singer Electronics, Akron, Ohio. As specialist in metal joining technology, developed solderability test for printed circuit boards, acceptable by Military for inclusion in official specification standards. Served as liaison engineer and trouble shooter on metal joining and related problems in all eastern company branches. Thorough working knowledge with all forms of non-destructive testing, including ultrasonic.

1965/1968

<u>WELDING ENGINEER</u>, Research Div., Arco Steel Co., Detroit, Mich. Devised new methods of automatic welding operation, with saving of 25% of labor costs over previous techniques. Company expert on all welding methods—carbon and stainless steel, especially resistance welding and tubular products.

(continued on Page 2)

WELDING ENGINEER (page 1)

1963/1965   <u>ASSISTANT RESEARCH ENGINEER</u>, Abbott and Wilcox, Detroit, Mich.
On staff of Dr. D.L. Robinson, in experimental research on welding and brazing of refractory and exotic metals (Molybdenum, Zirconium, Zircalloy, Hafnium and Beryllium) and on effect of welds on stainless steel. Developed process for brazing a spiral in boiler tubes for high temperature applications.

EDUCATION: <u>B.S. Welding Engineering</u>, Ohio State University, 1963.
Five year curriculum included 1 year Electrical Engineering, 1 year Chemical Engineering, 2 years Mechanical Engineering Non-destructive Testing, Corrosion Studies.

PERSONAL:

Born 3/14/40	Health ....Excellent
Height .... 5'8"	Marital
Weight ...... 161 lbs.	Status .. Married, 1 child
	Finances ...... In good order

Willing to relocate.

Outside interests: Antique cars, sculpture, ceramics.
Active sports include tennis, swimming and hunting.

MEMBERSHIP: Institute of Printed Circuits
American Welding Society
International Association of Machinists

<u>REFERENCES ON REQUEST</u>

JANE DOE
000 East 68th Street
New York, N.Y. 00000
(212) WA 0-0000

```
┌─────────────────┐
│                 │
│                 │
│     PHOTO       │
│                 │
│                 │
│                 │
│                 │
└─────────────────┘
```

F A S H I O N   M O D E L

Better-wear Dresses and Coats

PERSONAL DATA:

Age 23, attractive, well educated, single
Height: 5'6" in stockinged feet
Weight: 110 lbs. (without restraining diets)
Bust 34"   Waist 24"   Hips 34 1/2"
Back to waist: 16";   Excellent posture

Daughter of well-known fashion photographer.

EXPERIENCE:

MODEL, showroom and fashion shows.   1973-Present
House of Kennington, 417 Fifth Avenue, New York, N.Y.
Importers of knits and manufacturers of designer dresses
and coats.

SKETCH ARTIST, part-time model.   1971-1973
Smith & Roth, Inc., 498 Seventh Avenue, New York, N.Y.
Manufacturers of youthful line of ladies dresses.

EDUCATION:

Washington Irving High School, New York, N.Y.
Textile Design and Fashion Illustration major.
June 1969.

Endicott Junior College, Beverly, Mass.
A.A. degree in Home Economics. B+ average.
June 1971.

Barbizon School of Modeling, New York, N.Y.
Completed 4-month evening course in Fashion Modeling.
April 1972.

INTERESTS:

Collect antiques.
Swimming, sewing, sketching, as time permits.

REFERENCES AND PORTFOLIO ON REQUEST

JANE DOE
000 Greene Street
New York, N.Y. 10000
(000) WA 0-0000

. . . .

CAREER OBJECTIVE

Private Investigator for law firm or detective agency.

WORK EXPERIENCE

April to June
1974

Municipal Police Department, Flint, Michigan

Investigate all matters involving juveniles under age of
17: interviewing, data gathering, telephone interviews,
probate court attendance with juveniles in custody, preparation of cases for trial.

January to March
1974

Municipal Police Department, Detroit, Michigan

Investigate all crimes involving women of all ages and
crimes committed against women by males under 17 years
of age; interviewing, compiling data, observance of
living conditions, preparation of cases for trial.

Summer 1972
"   1973

American Telephone Company, New York, N.Y.

As Special Services Assistant, investigated all security
matters involving personnel or equipment--internal security, credit frauds, misuse of company property, preparation
of cases for trial, attendance at court proceedings, telephone interviews.

EDUCATION

School of Police Administration, Michigan University
B.S. degree in Law Enforcement, June 1974.

Relevant courses---Administrative Law Enforcement, Police
Patrol Administration, Criminal Investigation, Retail Store
Security, Legal Psychology, Police Science Laboratory,
Criminal Law, Highway Traffic Administration, Surveillance,
Evidence and Criminal Procedure.

St. Mary's High School, Brooklyn, N.Y.
Science major; graduated with honors, June 1970

PERSONAL DATA

Age 22; single; excellent health; 5'6"; 125 lbs.
Father, former police officer, now deceased.
Hobbies - photography, swimming, karate.

JANE DOE
000 Beekman Place
New York, N.Y. 10000
(212) WA 0-0000

M U S I C   T H E R A P I S T

EDUCATION: University of Iowa, Iowa City, Iowa
        B.S. degree, 1974. Major in music, minor in psychology.
    High School of Music and Art, New York, N.Y.
        Diploma, 1970. Graduated top 10% of class.

Among college level music courses I have taken which relate
to my major field of study, are:
        Sightsinging and Dictation
        Harmony and Counterpoint
        Psychology of Music
        Music Literature for Children
        Music in Recreation and Therapy
        Training in Vocal Techniques
        Instrumental Musicology
        American Folk Music

In addition I have had more than 8 years of private instruction
in piano, guitar, recorder and accordion.

EXPERIENCE: (Summers and Part-time)

6/73 - 9/73   Educational Alliance, (Camp Eden) Troy, N.Y.
        Music Counselor for retarded children.

6/72 - 8/72   Hilltop Country Day School, Great Neck, N.Y.
        Nursery Counselor.

9/70 - 6/71   Music Workshop, Rosyln Heights, N.Y.
        Accordion Teacher, Receptionist.

6/70 - 8/70   Henry Street Settlement House, New York, N.Y.
        Volunteer Leader, Saturday Children's Trips.

PERSONAL: Date of Birth: 6/26/52
    Marital Status: Single
    Appearance: 5'2", 110 lbs.
    Health: Excellent
    Interests: Ballet, Writing, Sports
    Languages: Good command of Spanish and Italian

REFERENCES UPON REQUEST

JOHN DOE
000 Peachtree Lane
Durham, North Carolina 00000
(000) WA 0-0000

OCCUPATIONAL GOAL

RECREATION LEADER or ASSISTANT DIRECTOR: Major interest in a position
in the field of recreation, with opportunity for further specialization later.

PERSONAL DATA

Date of Birth ...... May 21, 1952   Health................Excellent
Height .... 6'1"   Marital Status .... Single
Weight .... 181 lbs.

EDUCATION

B.S., State College at Durham, North Carolina, 1974.
Major in Physical Education; minor in Recreation.

MAJOR COURSES	MINOR COURSES
Principles, Physical Education	Arts and Crafts
Individual and Dual Sports	Principles of Recreation
Team Sports	Evaluation of Numbers
Advanced Gymnastics	Organization and Administration
First Aid	Leadership Techniques
Corrective Education	Recreation in Hospital Setting
Aquatics (Life Saving)	Community Recreation
Kinesiology	Folk and Square Dancing

EXTRACURRICULAR ACTIVITIES

Intramural Director - Junior and Senior years.
Captain, Basketball Team - Senior year.

WORK EXPERIENCE

After school hours: Assistant Director, Father Leary's Boys Club, Durham, N.C.
In charge of playrooms and play areas. Coached major team sports. Taught
singing games, tag games and relay activities.

During summer months: Assistant Head Counselor, Topeka Hill Camp, Topeka,
N.C. In charge of all games and athletic activities for youngsters in the 8-to-
10 year age group. Supervised staff of nine junior counselors.

JANE DOE
000 West 73rd Street
New York, N.Y. 10000
(212) WA 0-0000

Licensed
DENTAL HYGIENIST

EDUCATION:

Grace Dodge Vocational High School, New York, N.Y.
Academic diploma, June 1971. Top 10% of class.
- Voted the "Girl with the Radiant Smile."

New York City Community College, Brooklyn, N.Y.
Associate degree, Dental Hygiene, June 1973.
- Active in various student organizations.

Courses included the following areas of technical study:

Oral Prophylaxis.......4 hrs	Oral Hygiene Practice.....12 hrs
Roentgenology.........2 "	Periodontics .... 2 "
Pharmacology ....2 "	Organic Chemistry .... 4 "
Microbiology ....4 "	Dental Anatomy .... 4 "
Oral Pathology ....4 "	Preventive Dentistry...... 4 "

Took special course in Office Practice--typing, filing, fundamental
bookkeeping, record keeping, dental reports.

Projected educational plans: further college work in the evening,
to earn B.S. degree.

EXPERIENCE:

Dental Assistant
Dr. Horace Larson, D.D.S., Periodontal Specialist, New York.

1973/date

- Office charge duties: I make appointments, mail checkup re-
minders to patients, keep records, do typing and office bookkeeping.
- Professional duties: I assist at the chair, sterilize instruments,
take and process X-rays, mix filling compounds, prepare solutions,
clean teeth.

- Reason for desiring change: prefer to broaden my experience
to encompass general practice, eventually to work in public health
or school dental care program.

PERSONAL:

Age 22; Height 5'5"; Weight 118 lbs.; Excellent health.
- Good speaking voice; Endowed with perfect teeth.
- Like to be with people, happy disposition.
- Engaged, husband-to-be is Columbia medical student.

EDUCATION:

Columbia University School of Social Work (1972, 1973)
Graduate Seminars in Supervision
Smith College School of Social Work - M.S.W. degree (1964)
Field work: Children's Hospital, Boston, Mass.
Hunter College - B.A. degree in Sociology (1962)
Phi Beta Kappa; Student Development Committee

PROFESSIONAL EXPERIENCE:

1971-1973   N.Y. Foster Home & Adoption Service, New York.
Title: Casework Supervisor
Responsibilities: Supervised five social workers;
organized in-service training seminars.

1968-1971   DeWitt Children's Home, Meriden, Connecticut.
Title: Senior Social Worker
Responsibilities: Casework with children and
families; supervised student unit in social work.

1964-1968   New York University Medical Center, New York.
Title: Caseworker, Pediatric Service
Responsibilities: Casework, in-patient and out-
patient pediatrics service.

PRE-PROFESSIONAL AND VOLUNTEER EXPERIENCE:

1973-1974   Service with VISTA, husband-and-wife team.
Indian Reservation, New Mexico.

1960-1961   Counselor, Camp Hidalgo, Bound Brook, N.J.
Camp for underprivileged children.

MEMBERSHIP IN PROFESSIONAL ORGANIZATIONS:

National Association of Social Workers
American Personnel and Guidance Association

PERSONAL INFORMATION:

Born May 4, 1942;   Height 5'3";   Weight 118 lbs.
Health excellent;   Married, no children

Special interests: music, hiking, painting,
Active in local civic and community affairs.

Curriculum Vitae of

Curriculum Vitae of

JOHN DOE
000 Grand Concourse
Bronx, N.Y. 10468
(212) WA 0-0000

EDUCATIONAL BACKGROUND

St. John's University – B.S., 1946
Teachers College, Columbia University – M.A., 1947
State University of New York – Certificate, 1954
New York University – 30 credits towards Ed.D.

TEACHING AND SUPERVISORY EXPERIENCE

<u>High School of Art and Design</u>, New York, N.Y. Began teaching career in 1954 as one of eight charter members (with four art teachers and 65 students) at a newly organized school, the New York School of Industrial Art, presently known as the High School of Art and Design.

Helped to expand art department to a present force of close to 65 art teachers, with more than 2,000 students. The school is now rated as the top-ranking art high school in the United States.

For the past 15 years have served in a supervisory position as Department Chairman.

<u>Other Educational Institutions</u> – Conducted evening trade courses in lettering, design and silk screen as extension program for adults and as in-service courses for teachers, at the New York Evening School of Industrial Art.

TEACHING CERTIFICATES

Holder of four N.Y.C. Board of Education licenses:
    Hand Decorated Fabrics
    Sign and Showcard Lettering
    Commercial Art
    Department Chairman, Vocational Art

Frequently serve as Assistant Examiner for the New York City Board of Education, preparing and administering (singly or in committee) teaching examinations for license in Sign and Showcard, Fashion Illustration, Costume Design, and Commercial Art.

GUEST LECTURER

Featured speaker on silk screen, graphic arts and package design at numerous educational and professional organizations: Teachers College, American Institute of Graphic Arts; Screen Process Printing Association, Club of Printing House Craftsmen, the Navigators.

TRADE AFFILIATIONS

Concurrent with career in teaching and supervision, have retained active affiliation with industry, principally as Production Manager and Consultant for the Acme Paint Print Process Co., one of New York's leading designers and producers of silk screen displays, posters and point-of-sale advertising.

PUBLICATIONS

Author of more than 10 books, covering wide spectrum of graphic arts, advertising, and career guidance, many of which have been adopted by art schools and colleges throughout the country. Partial listing includes:

    Careers and Opportunities in Commercial Art
    Silk Screen Production Techniques
    Poster Design
    ABC of Lettering
    Art Directors' Work Book of Type Faces
    Careers and Opportunities in Teaching
    Silk Screen as a Fine Art

Have written for nearly every graphic arts and advertising publication in the United States. Partial listing includes:

    Signs of the Times (monthly feature on type design)
    Graphic Arts Monthly
    Lithographers Journal
    American Printer
    School Arts
    American Artist Magazine

JOHN DOE
000 Bank Street
New York, N.Y. 10000
(212) WA 0-0000

Age: 36
Hgt: 6'3"   Wgt: 195 lbs.
Health: Excellent
Married, 2 children

OBJECTIVE: PRINCIPAL or HEADMASTER of prep or military academy in New England area. Seek position in suburban school with limited student enrollment. Non-sectarian.
(Available beginning September 1975)

EDUCATION: Candidate for doctoral degree at Columbia University. Presently attending full time to complete dissertation. Expect Ed.D to be conferred June, 1975.

The City College of the State of New York, M.S. 1965.
North Texas State College, B.S., Physical Education, 1963.

PROFESSIONAL
EXPERIENCE: As a licensed teacher of health education in one of New York City's junior high schools (1100 boys and girls, 12 to 15 years of age) inaugurated successful physical fitness program, which has become the model for many of the district schools, both on the junior and senior high school level. The Education page of the New York Times recently carried a feature story in praise of this program.

Introduced a highly successful series of weekly assembly programs and after-school play activities. As teacher-coordinator working in close cooperation with community groups and parent-teacher association, activated better community participation, increasing membership by 150%.

During 7-week protracted illness of regular appointed Assistant Principal served as Acting Assistant Principal, with supervisory responsibilities for 43 teachers. My duties involved supervision of instruction, orientation of new teachers, requisition of supplies and equipment, and coordination of all faculty committees. Letters of recommendation attest to the quality of performance of these additional duties.

MILITARY: U.S. Air Force, 1957-1959. Separated from military with rank of 1st Lieutenant. Honorable discharge.

OUTSIDE
INTERESTS: All sports, folk dancing, horseback riding, mountain climbing. Inveterate reader. Active participation in civic and community organizations.

JANE DOE
000 Hewlett Road
Hewlett, N.Y. 10000
(212) WA 0-0000

· ·

LEGAL EDUCATION:

LL.B. degree, June 1974
Columbia University School of Law

Honors: American Civil Liberties Law Scholarship (2 years); American Jurisprudence Prize
for Excellence in Procedure.

PRE-LEGAL EDUCATION:

B.S. degree in Economics, June 1971
Cornell University, Ithaca, New York

Honors: Summa Cum Laude; Dean's List;
Tuition financed with Regents Scholarship.

Extracurricular Activities: Red Cross Volunteer
Aide, Secretary, Pre-Bar Society; Member,
International Students Association.

WORK EXPERIENCE:

Summer months, 1969 to 1973

Practising Law Institute
20 Vesey Street, New York, N.Y.
Proofreading, cite checking, editing

Port Authority Legal Department
111 Eighth Avenue, New York, N.Y.
Typing, legal research, secretarial work

International Brotherhood of Electrical
Workers, Local 1212
150 Fifth Avenue, New York, N.Y.
Typing contracts, general clerical work

Macy's Department Store
Herald Square, New York, N.Y.
Clerical work, Claims & Adjustment Dep't.

PERSONAL DATA:

Born May 14, 1950; Single; Excellent Health
Height 5'4"; Weight 120 lbs.
Father, Tax Consultant

JOHN DOE
000 Evans Street
Santa Barbara, Calif. 90000
(213) WA 0-0000

S Y N O P S I S

OPERATIONS ANALYST-ECONOMETRICIAN. Experience includes development of econometric models for management and logistic systems; economic analysis; transportation
systems; coal mining electric power generation techniques; urban growth patterns;
disarmament; R&D planning and long-range company resource planning.

Experience also encompasses engineering design; quality control; reliability and
R&D in the field of astronautics.

EDUCATION

Ph. D. Economics, University of California, Berkeley (1962)
Fields of Specialization: Mathematical Statistics; Economic
Theory; Business Cycles; Industrial Organization; Marketing.
Dissertation: The Psychology of Rationality
Honors: 4-year Fellowship in Economic Statistics (1957-1960)

B.A., School of Business Administration, Northwestern Univer-
sity, Evanston, Illinois (1955)
Major in business finance with minor in mathematics
Honors: Four years on Dean's List

EXPERIENCE

MEMBER OF PROFESSIONAL STAFF, Warner Electronics, Santa
Barbara, California. (July 1970 to present.)

Currently Assistant Project Leader on multi-million dollar
management study of Navy Material Support Establishment.
Responsible for a multi-echelon logistics support model using
econometric techniques.

Other work at Warner Electronics: Econometric model of a
General Electric Company component having two billion sales
per year; economic analyses of U.S. railroad transportation
system; coal mining; electric power generation techniques;
urban growth patterns; feasible policies for adaptation to
disarmament; several classified studies.

PROJECT ADMINISTRATOR, Advanced Product Planning Department,
Astro-Dynamics, San Diego, California (June 1964 to July 1969)

Development of new system concepts; R&D planning; long range
company resource planning.

Other work at Astro-Dynamics: Astronautics. Progressed from Quality Control Engineer to Design Specialist; responsible for development of destructive and non-destructive test programs; experimental designs; consultation with engineering groups; development of test and reliability programs on all project proposals.

ASSISTANT PROFESSOR OF BUSINESS ADMINISTRATION, Palo Alto University, Palo Alto, Calif. (September 1961 to June 1964.)

Taught courses in Economic Statistics, Marketing, Business Policy. Consulted with various firms on such topics as: prediction of airline traffic density; retail store layout; product strategy for a small company; pricing policies.

SPECIAL LECTURER ON BUSINESS ADMINISTRATION, University of Texas, Austin, Texas (September 1960 to September 1961.)

Delivered series of lectures on Marketing, Price Policies, Business Economics, Retail Store Management.

PROFESSIONAL AFFILIATIONS

American Economic Association
Institute of Mathematical Statistics
American Mathematical Society
American Institute of Aeronautics and Astronautics

PUBLICATIONS AND PAPERS

R&D Resource Estimation and Incentive Contracting: Some Production Function Considerations, paper presented at the Institute of Management Science National Meeting, San Francisco, 1971.

Planning a Least Cost Reliability Constrained Development Program: A Capacitated Network Approach, paper presented at First Annual Meeting, American Institute of Aeronautics and Astronautics, Washington, D.C., July 1970.

Currently collaborating on college text on Econometrics.

PERSONAL

Born August 1, 1932   Married, two children   Excellent health

JOHN DOE
000 Stuart Road
Easton, Pa. 60000
(000) WA 0-0000

PHYSICAL CHEMISTRY / ELECTRON AND LIGHT MICROSCOPY

EDUCATION:

University of California, Berkeley, Calif. --------------- 1969
    M.S., Physical Chemistry
Lehigh University, Bethlehem, Pa. --------------------- 1967
    B.S., Chemistry and Mathematics
Rensselaer Polytechnic Institute, Troy, N.Y. ------------ 1972
    Course in Metallurgical Electron Microscopy
Northeastern University, Boston, Mass. --------------- 1971
    Course in Metallurgical Electron Microscopy

EXPERIENCE:

ANALYTICAL CHEMIST, Chas. H. Pfizer & Co., Easton, Pa.
1969 to Present
    In charge of Electron and Light Microscopy Laboratory and
Physical Testing Laboratory. Work involves selection and
installation of high resolution electron microscope, scanning
electron microscope, vacuum evaporator for surface replication,
electron diffraction equipment and a phase contrast-interference
contrast optical microscope, in addition to all supporting equipment and facilities.
    With these instruments have actively participated in the
development of unusual powder metal alloys, metallic pigments,
high purity metal strip, magnetic pigments, ferrites, ceramic
raw materials, extender pigments and novel paper coating pigments.

ASSISTANT CHEMIST, Zenith Chemical Corp., Berkeley, Calif.
1967 to 1970 (Part-time)
    Work involved wet and instrumental analysis of iron oxides,
chromium oxides, and minerals.

PROFESSIONAL AFFILIATIONS:

American Chemical Society
National Association of Physical Chemists

PERSONAL:

Age 32; Height 6'2"; Weight 190 lbs.; Married, 3 children
Veteran, U.S. Army; Honorable Discharge 1963

BIOCHEMIST - LIFE SCIENTIST

JOHN DOE
000 Iowa Road
New Haven, Conn. 30000
(000) WA 0-0000

EDUCATION:

University of Southern California
    Ph.D., Biochemistry 1962
    M.S., Biochemistry 1957
    B.A., Zoology 1955
Marquette University
    Medicine, Postdoctoral 1968

EXPERIENCE:

1969 - Date

United Aircraft Corporation, Windsor Locks, Conn.
SENIOR SCIENTIST - Preparation of man to function in foreign environments. Authored: Substitution of Pulmonary Ventilation for Breathing - NASA Contract. Wrote and submitted "Urine Fuel Cell" to Office of Naval Research and U.S. Army. Prepared for U.S. Army, "Detection of Personnel by Chemical Means." Worked on MORL (Manned Orbital Research Lab), PIAPACA (Psychological Acquisition Processing and Control System), ECLLS (Environmental Control Lunar Landing System). Problems of water management and life support. Proposal on EXOBIOLOGY submitted to NASA, Washington.

1957 - 1968

Applied Biol. Sciences Lab., Inc., Glendale, Calif.
RESEARCH DIRECTOR - Supervision of study on blood enzymes under contract from U.S. Army Medical Research and Development.

Cedars of Lebanon Hospital, Los Angeles, Calif.
RESEARCH BIOCHEMIST - Excretion of bile pigments. Institute of Public Health grant.

Saint Joseph Hospital, Los Angeles, Calif.
CHIEF CLINICAL BIOCHEMIST - Supervised and developed all biochemical procedures.

California Gland Company, Vernon, Calif.
CONSULTANT - Biochemical Analysis.

East Los Angeles Junior College, Los Angeles, Calif.
INSTRUCTOR - Chemistry.

Marquette University, Milwaukee, Wis.
RESEARCH ASSOCIATE and student.

University of Southern California, Los Angeles, Calif.
RESEARCH ASSISTANT and student.

PERSONAL:

Born June 10, 1934, Los Angeles, California.
Married, one child.

Curriculum Vitae of

JANE DOE
46 Simonson Place
Staten Island, N.Y. 10302
(212) WA 0-0000

EDUCATION

M.S. degree in Physiology, June 1970, University of Massachusetts
B.A. degree in Biology, June 1968, Niagara University

Undergraduate Studies

General Physiology
Microbiology
Histology
Microtechnique
Organic Chemistry
Biochemistry
Genetics
Cell Physiology
General Physics
Mammalian Anatomy

Graduate Studies

Mammalian Physiology
Endocrine Physiology
Electron Microscopy
Physiological Genetics
Microbiological Physiology
Biophysics
Special Project (involving
oculomotor physiology)
Transplantation Immunology
Statistics

WORK EXPERIENCE

Research Associate (Jan. 1972 to Present)

Neurology Department, Columbia University College of Physicians and Surgeons,
New York, N.Y.

Field of Study: Muscle contraction in normal and dystropic mice;
Effects of series of tetanii.

Job Duties: Use of Tektronic dual beam oscilloscopes, Grass stimulators
and other electronic equipment; Fine dissection work; Oscilloscope trace
photography; Statistical evaluation of data; Physiological testing on
patients using Grass and Schwarzer equipment; Electrophysiological recording during cryosurgery on Parkinsonians.

Research Assistant (Sept. 1970 to Dec. 1971)

Pathology Department, Francis Delafield Hospital, Columbia University Medical
Center, New York, N.Y.

Field of Study: Endocrine tumors and leukemia in rats and mice.

Job Duties: Mammalian investigations including surgery, autopsy, tumor transfers, virus passage, breeding; immunoelectrophoresis and other immunochemical techniques.

Graduate Teaching Assistant (Sept. 1969 to June 1970)

Physiology Department, University of Massachusetts, Amherst, Mass. Assistant to Professor Wilbur H. Brown.

Job Duties: Laboratory preparation and supervision; examination, supervision and grading for introductory course in General Physiology.

───────────── PROFESSIONAL SOCIETIES ─────────────

Member of:
    American Society for Physiologists
    American Association for Advancement of Sciences
    American Association of University Women

───────────── PERSONAL INFORMATION ─────────────

Born: 3/16/47 in Paris, France; came to United States at age 10.
Languages: Speak, read and write French fluently; working knowledge of German and Russian.
Hobbies: Photography, skiing, theater.
Father: Professor of Economics, University of Illinois.

Curriculum Vitae
of

_____

JOHN DOE, M.D.
000 West 68th Street
New York, N.Y. 10000
(212) WA 0-0000

_____

─────────────── PROFESSIONAL GOAL ───────────────

To participate in a program which provides good
medical care to the indigent and underprivileged.

─────────────── EDUCATIONAL BACKGROUND ───────────────

1959......1963 Columbia University, New York; B.A. degree.

1963......1967 Johns Hopkins School of Medicine, Maryland; M.D. degree

1967......1968 Beth Israel Hospital, New York; Rotating Internship.

1968......1971 Roosevelt Hospital, New York; Three-year Residency.
                2 years.....internal medicine
                1 year .....hematology

─────────────── MILITARY SERVICE ───────────────

1971......1973 Captain, Army Medical Corps; Fort Carson, Colorado.
                Primarily in-patient service at base hospital
                with 6 to 8 hours per week out-patient duty.
                Honorable discharge, Sept. 1973.

─────────────── PROFESSIONAL BACKGROUND ───────────────

1973......1974 Out-patient Clinic, ILGWU Medical Center, New York.
                Served as examining physician for union members
                and their dependants.

1974......Date U.S. Public Health Service Hospital, New York.
                Cancer research, primarily in leukemia and other
                related diseases.

─────────────── ADDITIONAL INFORMATION ───────────────

Birth Date: June 18, 1943   Height: 5'10"   Weight: 170 lbs.
Health: Excellent   Married, no children

Currently in the process of studying for boards in internal medicine.

JOHN DOE   000 FAIRMONT AVENUE, STATEN ISLAND, N.Y. 10314   (212) 727-0000

PHOTOGRAPHIC TECHNICIAN

WORK EXPERIENCE

Jerry Korman Photographer, Staten Island, N.Y.   <u>Staff Foreman</u>
In charge of color work and die transfer department, supervising staff
of 6 assistants.   (1971-Present)

Stanford Photo Co., New York, N.Y.   <u>Assistant Technician</u>
Photofinishing and distribution of color material.   (1968-1971)

Photolettering Service Inc., New York, N.Y.   <u>Paste-up artist</u>
Photolettering composition, visual spacing and working directly from
layouts provided by the art department for leading advertising
agencies.   (1964-1968)

Burr Photo Laboratory, New York, N.Y.   <u>Darkroom Technician</u>
Retouching fashion photo negatives with pencil and airbrush, involving considerable art skills.   (1962-1964)

EDUCATION

American School of Photography, Newark, N.J.
Completed 2-year course in b/w and color work   June, 1962

High School of Art and Design, New York, N.Y.
Graduated 1960 with major in commercial photography and graphic
arts. Valedictorian of class; winner of Scholastic Magazine
photography award.

New York University, (evenings).
Advanced courses in photocomposition and introductory course in
cinematography.

PUBLISHED WORK

Have published several articles on new developments in the field of
color photography in the Photographic Journal, Popular Photography
and Mechanics Illustrated. A number of my photographs were used
to illustrate fashion articles in Woman's Wear Daily.

PERSONAL

Age - 33   Height - 5'11"   Weight - 180 lbs.   Health - Excellent
Wife employed as assistant editor for book publishing firm.

REFERENCES AND PORTFOLIO ON REQUEST

John Doe   000 Charles Avenue, Staten Island, New York 10302   (212) 933-0000

FINANCIAL ANALYST TO OVERSEAS-BASED COMPANY

PERSONAL: Age – 30   Height – 6'0"   Weight – 175 lbs.   Health – Excellent
                   Marital Status – Married, no children

EDUCATION: MBA Finance, Columbia University, New York, June 1969
                   Top quarter of class.

                   BA History, Wesleyan University, Connecticut, June 1967
                   Activities: Fraternity Vice President, Intramural sports.
                   Financed 50% through summer and part-time employment.
                   Linguistic abilities in French, German and Spanish.

MILITARY: LIEUTENANT, U.S. NAVY, Sept. 1969 to Sept. 1972
                   In charge of supply department (25 men) on a destroyer escort.

                   Collateral duties:
                   Financial Manager for ship. Annual operating budget totalled
                   $125,000.
                   Inventory Manager for 18,000 different repair parts valued at
                   $150,000.
                   Designed and implemented audit for control of financial and
                   stock record accuracy.
                   Consolidated financial and inventory management offices
                   into one facility.

                   Several times winner of special citations.

EXPERIENCE: Continental Manufacturing Company, New York, N.Y.
                   SENIOR FINANCIAL ANALYST for eight overseas affiliates with
Oct. 1972   combined annual sales of $60 million and net profit of $2.3
   to   million.
Present
                   Evaluated annual and five-year profit plans. Interpreted trends
                   of business and overall market.

                   Published quarterly in-depth commentaries analyzing variances
                   from plan and last year.

                   Determined timing, content and format of profit plans, sales
                   reports, and financial statements. Co-designed standardized
                   international reporting format to be implemented in July of this
                   year.

REFERENCES: Available upon request.

JOHN DOE
000 St. John's Avenue
Lakewood, N.J. 08615
(201) 933-0000

<u>ARCHITECT</u>
Licensed, State of New York

———————————— PROFESSIONAL SCOPE ————————————

To affiliate with innovative architectural firm specializing in the planning,
designing and construction of shopping center malls in newly developing
suburban communities.

———————————————— EXPERIENCE ————————————————

(1971 to Present)   Assistant to supervising architect, Reis, Lawson &
Robbins, Lakewood, N.J., a firm employing staff of 35 which includes surveyors, team
of designers, detail draftsmen, urban marketing researchers, planning architects and
engineers.

My responsibilities include conferring with clients,
recommending designs to meet their specific requirements; document study of zoning
laws and building codes, assist in coordinating work of planning architects and staff
engineers; oversee constructing, coordinating efforts of team of four junior architects.

(1968 to 1971)   Staff architect, Ardmore-Fields Associates, New
York, N.Y.

Served as liaison with architects, designers, manage-
ment consultants, and construction engineers. Was co-recipient of Architectural League's
annual award for outstanding work of young architects and designers.

———————————— PROFESSIONAL TRAINING ————————————

Columbia University, School of Architecture, 5 year course, B.S. 1968
Mechanics Institute, evening course in structural design (at present)

————————————————— PERSONAL —————————————————

Age: 29   Height: 5'10"   Weight: 161 lbs.   Health: Excellent
Marital Status: Married, wife is freelance package designer, 1 child
Finances: Good, live within my means, no outstanding debts
                  Rent 6-room house, own car and stationwagon
Hobbies: Camping, painting, ceramics
Relocation: No problem

———————————— PROFESSIONAL AFFILIATIONS ————————————

Member: American Institute of Architects
                  National Association of Interior Designers
                  Architectural League of New York

ARCHITECT

JOHN DOE
000 Rochambeau Avenue
New York, N.Y. 10000
(212) 933-0000

OBJECTIVE

Full or part-time position in the field of development and production of audio visual presentations.

EXPERIENCE

1970-Date   Freelance consultant for special audio visual projects, New York City Transit Authority Training Center.

1964-1970   In charge of audio visual department, Transit Authority Car Maintenance Training Center.
Trained employees in the many crafts of the transit industry, developed various types of visuals, such as viewgraphs, training books, cinema, training posters and sound synchronized slide and film strip lectures.
Researched, developed the structure and wrote the script. Did the photography, graphics and sound to complete each project.

In 1968, received a fourth citation and $500 award from the N.Y.C. Suggestion Program, for the development of S.O.P. Training Booklets, the use of which reduced job orientation time by more than one-third. This resulted in a saving of nearly $80,000 for the program.

Retired from active service in 1970.

1941-1964   Began as a Helper in the car maintenance department of the N.Y.C. Board of Transportation (later Transit Authority). Took promotion exams and moved up to Car Inspector, Foreman, Assistant Supervisor. As Supervisor, was in charge of 60 maintainers and helpers.

Received three merit awards from the Transit Authority for improvements in processes and work techniques.

Parallel with my work at the Transit Authority, did freelance photography and experimental work in photo equipment, evenings and weekends.

Was granted several patents from the U.S. Patent Office; one of them for an automatic diaphragm control device for single lens reflex cameras. This was put into production and was written up in several photography journals.

1939-1941   A&T Commercial Refrigeration Co., New York City. Installed and maintained refrigeration systems in display fixtures and walk-in coolers for the food industry.

1931-1939   Eastern Golf Co., New York City.
Did bench work in the manufacture of golf balls. (Part
and full time, depending on school requirements.)
Helped to finance my way through schools.

EDUCATION

1937-1939   N.Y.U. School of Engineering, with special
courses in heating, ventilating and air conditioning
engineering. Graduated 1939.

1933-1936   College of the City of New York; general
arts program with courses in creative writing, social
science, mathematics.

1930-1933   Stuyvesant High School, New York City.
Member of Arista Honor Society, fencing team, soccer
team. Graduated with awards in art and science.

SPECIAL
TRAINING

1965-1968   Completed Transit Authority-sponsored courses
in: Principles of Management and Administration (N.Y.C.
Board of Education); Programmed Instruction (Columbia
University School of Education); Cinematography (New
School for Social Research).

1939-1940   Stuyvesant Evening High Certificate (Federal
Manpower Training Program) in Machine Shop practice.

1936-1937   Technicians Institute, New York City,
Commercial Refrigeration; 1 year.

Presently attending City University towards degree in
Industrial Cinematography.

PERSONAL

Born April 20, 1914; Height 5'9";   Weight 195 lbs.
Health - Excellent; last medical checkup in January 1975.
Marital Status - Married; three children.
Finances - Very good. Own car, several top grade cameras
and related equipment, complete photo lab and home machine
and tool shop.
Interests - Hiking, painting, photography and development
of instrumentation, relating to audio visual field.

References Available

JOHN DOE
000 Green Street
Detroit, Michigan 72205
(706) 933-0000 PHOTOCOMPOSITION SUPERVISOR

EMPLOYMENT HISTORY

8/72 - present Paccaro Corp., Detroit, Mich.
Computerized typesetting house

PRODUCTION COORDINATOR/PLANNER. In the main, duties entail typographic make-up of college and technical texts, following client specifications; overseeing the work through inputting, computer composition, typesetting, proofreading and correction cycles. Responsible for the total production of any given text. Utilize IBM 370/135, OS multiprogram environment and a Harris Fototronic photocomposer. Have working knowledge of Basic Assembly Language (BAL) and COBOL.

6/70 - 8/72 Graphics, Inc., Detroit, Mich.
Computerized Phototypesetters

SUPERVISOR OF COMPUTER OPERATIONS. Duties entailed scheduling and running an IBM 360/40, DOS, single partition computer and an RCA Videocomp 800 photocomposer, coordinating the various aspects of page makeup, programming, correction cycles, data manipulations and photocomposing. Also, analyzing data for programming--i.e. for fielding, edit insert, etc., as well as designing and implementing forms for tape logs, production controls and job run sheets.
        Was originally hired to set up and supervise the Proofreading Department. After becoming familiarized with the computerization aspect of cold type production, was promoted to position of Formatter with substantial increase in salary.

9/69 - 6/70 Detroit Daily Press
Newspaper Publication

EDITORIAL ASSISTANT. Worked as proofreader on the lobster shift, while in my junior and senior years at Detroit University. Acquired a working knowledge of the fundamentals of hot metal newspaper typography and production.

PERSONAL HISTORY

Age - 28; Height - 5'8"; Weight - 145 lbs.; Health - excellent
Married - one child; four brothers in family, all in printing field.

EDUCATION

B.A., English Literature, Detroit University, June 1970.
Completed Systems Analysis Course, Merrill School, 1971.

Section **3**

QUESTIONS THE INTERVIEWER MAY ASK

A résumé is often referred to as a passport to a job interview. The interview, in turn, may be said to serve the same function in regard to the actual job for which you hope to be hired. Hardly ever—it would perhaps be more correct to say *never*—is anyone hired for any responsible position without the formality of a face-to-face meeting with the prospective employer, who will want to see firsthand how you, the applicant, measure up in relation to claims you make on the résumé.

Remember, your prospective employer at this stage of the negotiations has evidently evinced an interest in your professional qualifications or else you would not have been invited for the interview. What the interviewer wants to check out now are specific points of information to supplement and/or support your claims—documentary material, a portfolio of samples if you are a commercial artist or fashion model, sales records if you are applying for a selling job, critical reviews if you are in the performing arts, letters of recommendation and communications from previous employers or anyone else who can attest to your experience, and other factual data. And an equally important consideration in a total estimate of you· as a prospective employee is the evaluation of you as a person —your general appearance, grooming, manner of speaking, your attitude during the interview, general behavior and other subtle character traits that show you to be a person who is easy to get along with, one who is cooperative, ambitious and trustworthy. In short, are you the type of person who is likely to become an asset to the company?

Rehearse These Top Ten

Here are some questions that almost inevitably come up during most job interviews. It would be wise to go over these questions (with corresponding answers) in your mind. Better still, rehearse them on a recorder, or with the help of a friend act out the part of the prospective employer, before you set forth on the actual interview.

Why do you want to join our company?

Your answer should include something to the effect that you have acquainted yourself with the company's history, products and services, and feel confident that you can make a contribution to the growth of the company because of your special qualifications.

Tell me something about your previous employment?

If you've held down a number of jobs in the past, confine yourself to the last few positions, highlighting your duties, responsibilities, and achievements. If you are a youngster with limited work experience, include summer and part-time employment as well. If you are just out of school, show how your extracurricular activities while attending school have a bearing on the job you are applying for.

How did your previous employers treat you?

"Fairly and squarely," should be your reply if that is really true. If the facts do not warrant that simple reply, you may briefly explain the situation, without recrimination or going into particulars.

Why did you leave your last job?

Briefly state your reason for leaving but at no time give the impression that you are a malcontent by referring to personality clashes with previous employers. Don't tell a sad tale of how you were made an innocent victim of nepotism, prejudice or gross unfairness. If you have left your previous employer to seek greater opportunities for growth and advancement, then by all means say so.

How old are you?

Here is a ticklish question. You might be tempted to "adjust" your age to suit the age level that you think the employer is looking for. If you haven't been truthful about your age, the person interviewing you may suspect (with some justification) that other things you have said about yourself may also be untrue. Then, too, giving an incorrect age has been known to cause complications later in matters pertaining to social security, pension rights, health insurance, etc. If, for whatever reason, you prefer not to give your exact age at this stage of the employment negotiations, it's best to speak in terms of a general age level such as "over 30," "over 40," and so on. Obviously, a response like "over 21" is not especially helpful—nor readily believable—if you have reached an age of 50 or so. The reply "over 21" may sound irritatingly flippant or outright evasive to an interviewer who feels the question to be a valid one for the particular job you are seeking.

In every instance, whether in the matter of age or other pertinent facts, the truth is best.

What salary do you expect?

Try not to commit yourself too early in the interview proceedings to specifying a definite salary. Instead, tactfully defer the matter until you know more about the duties and responsibilities entailed in the position you are applying for. Find out whether the company has an established policy in regard to a fixed salary schedule for your particular job classification. Unless you know these facts, you may be way off beat in the salary you ask for. You may name a salary that is too low, in which case you actually undersell yourself and your true worth. On the other hand, if the salary you name is too high, you may price yourself out of the picture.

It is perhaps better to state a *range* rather than a fixed amount. Sometimes it is more expedient to mention the terminal salary of your last job and use that as a basis for negotiation for the job under consideration.

What are your future career plans?

Try to show how the job you are presently applying for fits in with your long-range career goal. Also discuss plans you have or are willing to make in preparation for professional advancement in your field. Allude to courses you are now taking or hope to take, your professional affiliations and in-service training for which you hope to qualify.

How do you spend your spare time?

How a person spends his spare time can serve as a clue to his character and personality. Your interviewer would want to know something about the kind of books you enjoy reading, sports and hobbies you are interested in, or your professional and civic affiliations. If possible, link your spare-time activities and cultural pursuits with the job you are being interviewed for.

Don't you think you are too young (or too old) to take on a job with such responsibilities?

In reply to a question concerning your youthfulness, you may point out that you feel all the more qualified for the job *because* of your youth. Show how, in your estimation, the responsibilities of the position, as outlined by the interviewer, can be handled best by a young person like yourself—one who can face the challenge with the youthful vigor and vision the job calls for. Organize your answer and phrase it in such a way as to present your youth as a positive asset, not as an acceptable defense.

Similarly, if the interviewer questions your aptitude for the job because you are too old, point out how your long experience and previous success on jobs with similar responsibilities qualify you. Show how effectively you will be able to carry out your responsibilities because you possess the mature judgment and experience that the job obviously calls for.

In either case, phrase your answer so that your age turns out to be a strategic advantage rather than an obvious shortcoming.

Are you taking any courses?

If you are presently taking courses, be prepared to show how they relate to the position you are applying for and how they will help to advance you professionally. If you are not enrolled in any courses at present, you may want to discuss your plans for future study.

More Practice Questions

Now, let's see how you would phrase answers to questions such as these:

1. Tell me something about yourself?
2. At school, what courses did you like best; which ones did you like least?
3. What one person had the greatest influence on your life, and why?
4. Why did you choose this particular field of work?
5. How did you finance yourself through school?
6. How did you rate scholastically in your senior year?
7. Where do you hope to be five years from now—and ten years from now? What is your ultimate professional goal?
8. What prompted you to apply for a job with our company?
9. How do you feel about your family—and about marriage?
10. How many dependents do you have?
11. What, in your estimation, is the key to professional success?
12. Are you looking for a permanent or temporary job?
13. What is your concept of the ideal boss?
14. Do you have friends or relations working for our company?
15. Have you ever been in trouble with the law?
16. Are you free to travel? Would you be willing to relocate?
17. What in your opinion especially qualifies you for the job?
18. What books or magazines do you read?
19. Have you ever been fired from a job? If so, why?
20. Are you in a position to work overtime when necessary?
21. Have you been in the military service?
22. Do you suffer from any allergies or recurring illnesses?
23. What salary are you expecting?
24. Do you have any outstanding debts?
25. How far did you go in your formal education?
26. Do you think that this is the field of work you want to stay in?
27. How is your memory for names and faces?
28. Why did you leave your previous job?
29. Do you belong to any professional organizations?
30. Do you own your own home?
31. What do you know about the product and services of our company?
32. Are other members of your family in the same line of work?
33. Who are our competitors in the field?
34. Have you supervised people before? How many?
35. Have you ever been in business for yourself?
36. Do you aspire to start your own business some day?
37. What, in your opinion, is the value of a college education?
38. What foreign languages do you speak?
39. What traveling time would you have to allow to get to work?
40. What is your marital status?
41. How, in your opinion, will automation affect the future of our industry?

42. How would you react to working under the directions of a younger person?

43. What do you hope to do when you retire?

44. Are you continuing your education?

45. How do you spend your vacations?

46. Where did you get your professional training?

47. What sports do you excel in?

48. What, in your estimation, is the outstanding achievement in your life?

49. What are your pet peeves?

50. Is it all right to call your previous employer for reference?

Supplement this list with questions of your own, the kind *you* would ask the job applicant if you were the interviewer. Formulate answers to all of these questions verbally as well as mentally. Hear your own words; get used to the sound of your voice as you answer these questions, one by one. If you have a close friend who would agree to play the part of the interviewer, you'll be helped immeasurably. You can then go through a complete rehearsal—from the time you enter the office and in a friendly tone introduce yourself, to the time you thank the interviewer and leave the office. If you don't have anyone to cast for the part of the interviewer, you can act out both parts, using a tape recorder. The effect won't be as realistic, but it will help to attune your ears to the sound of the questions and the manner in which you answer them.

QUESTIONS YOU MAY ASK THE INTERVIEWER

Here are a few questions that you may want to ask the interviewer—questions that you can safely ask without appearing to be aggressively inquisitive. In fact, most interviewers will consider such questions a favorable index of your interest in the job and in the company.

1. Is this a permanent job or is it of a temporary or seasonal nature?

2. What is the policy of the company in regard to promotion from within the ranks?

3. Does the company have a training program in which I might participate?

4. Does the company have a pension or retirement system, hospitalization and insurance plans for its employees?

5. Does the company have a set schedule of salaries for the various job classifications?

6. Are salary increases based on merit, promotional examination or length of service?

7. How soon after the interview will I know whether I am hired?

INTERVIEW PITFALLS AND HOW TO AVOID THEM

Some time ago a survey was made by the Director of Placement at Northwestern University to determine the most common causes of failure in job interview situations. From actual records of interviews submitted by the personnel directors of over 150 large corporations, a list of 50 reasons was compiled. This list appeared in a very informative job-guidance booklet published under the auspices of the New York Life Insurance Company. Some of the most prevalent causes of failure indicated in the survey are listed here, with suggestions for eliminating them.

Poor personal appearance

You can't very well help it if nature has not endowed you with the handsome features and perfect figure of a popular movie star, but you *can* improve your grooming and neatness of appearance. Employment counselors agree that good grooming, appropriate dress, and care in body hygiene are major factors which consciously or subconsciously influence the prospective employer's personal reaction to the applicant.

Overbearing, overaggressive, conceited, superiority complex—"know-it-all" attitude

The interviewer is likely to respond negatively to the applicant who displays an arrogant "know-it-all" attitude. A confident, optimistic attitude is fine, but don't act the part of the pushy supersalesman. Let your record or samples of work speak for you.

Inability to express oneself clearly—poor voice, diction, grammar

Some authors of job-guidance books recommend that applicants take extensive speech lessons and put in hours of daily practice in speech drills; but, under the circumstances, that is unrealistic advice. When you are looking for a job, you can hardly be expected to have the time or the patience for elocution lessons. However, you *can* try to be more mindful of the way you speak. Get someone to listen to you who will point out shortcomings in your speech pattern, or listen to a playback of your voice on a recorder to help you improve your enunciation and diction.

Your general speech pattern will be helped immeasurably if you are well-prepared with ready answers to questions likely to come up during the interview.

Lack of planning for a career; no purpose or goal

The interviewer is bound to get an unfavorable impression of you if you have no clear idea of the kind of job you are looking for. If you say, "I can do anything," you reveal by your alleged versatility a lack of a specific objective. The interviewer will respect you more if you state in specific terms what you are capable of doing, and how it ties in with your long-range career goal.

Lack of confidence and poise, nervousness

Excessive nervousness and lack of confidence are deeply rooted emotional traits that even psychiatrists find difficult to correct. You can, however, make these personality shortcomings less noticeable by adequate prepara-

tion. This means preparing a well-organized résumé and thoroughly familiarizing yourself with it, as well as with answers to questions that the interviewer is likely to ask. Good grooming and proper dress also contribute to a feeling of confidence and poise.

Overemphasis on money

Don't give the impression that a big paycheck is your main interest and that it constitutes the only reason for your desire to work for the company. In your interview you will ultimately discuss salary, but you should do so discreetly by equating it with more cogent reasons for your interest in the job.

Poor scholastic standing—just got by

If you have not distinguished yourself scholastically, don't apologize for your educational shortcomings, but rather emphasize what you are doing presently to correct them. Tell what you are doing to upgrade your education —courses you are taking or plan to take, professional affiliations, cultural pursuits, etc.

Lack of courtesy—ill-mannered

Social amenities are as important in business as they are in personal relationships. "Thanks" and "please" are words easily found in the dictionary, but not used often enough. An interviewer instinctively is antagonistic to an applicant who shows poor manners or lack of courtesy.

Your general attitude and behavior are indicative of your personality and character. Most job counselors agree that good personal attributes are in many ways as important as technical proficiency. Some say they are even more so.

Failure to look interviewer in the eye

Strange, isn't it, that this should be listed as a common reason why some applicants fail the interview? Nonetheless it is true that the interviewer is inclined to have a vague distrust of an applicant who consistently evades his glance. He is left with the impression that the applicant is either not straightforward or, at best, is extremely shy and insecure.

When you are seated opposite the interviewer—or are involved in any two-way communication—put your "best face forward." Register interest in the conversation by directing your remarks and your gaze at the interviewer, not at the floor or ceiling, and listening intently in turn. Make the interviewer the center of your interest and attention.

Limp, fishy handshake

There is something about a limp, fishy handshake which suggests a lack of moral stamina. If the interviewer extends a hand, accept it as a gesture of good will and friendship. Respond with a firm grasp of your full hand, not merely your fingertips. But don't overdo the hearty handshake bit, by being a bone-crusher or hand-pumper.

Unhappy home life

If you are unhappy at home, can't get along with your parents, have been the victim of marital conflict, or have had a nervous breakdown, don't tell your interviewer all about it at the very first meeting. Such a background may mark you as a potential "security risk," someone with unresolved problems that may interfere with your duties on the job. If you aren't blessed with a happy personal life, don't bring up the subject, but if the interviewer does, then, of course, answer all questions honestly but without elaboration.

Sloppy application blank

An application blank with crossed-out writing, missing information, smudges, or fingerprints obviously militates against anyone applying for a position as accountant, secretary, commercial artist, or other occupations where accuracy and neatness are requisite work traits. But neatness and accuracy are important to varying degrees for any responsible position, and the appearance of your completed application serves as a graphic sampling of those attributes.

Job-hopping

Interviewers watch for symptoms of instability in the job applicant's history. If you have had a succession of short-duration jobs, it would seem to indicate that you do not know what type of work you want to do, that you lack persistence, or worse still, that you might have been dismissed from the multiple jobs you have held.

If, by chance or choice, you have had a number of short-duration jobs, don't elaborate on this phase of your work-experience record and erroneously identify yourself as a chronic job-hopper.

Cynical outlook

It is one of the interviewer's responsibilities to the employer to screen out the cynical applicant. A cynic can easily become a malcontent, and that is one step away from a trouble maker. Obviously such a person is no asset to any company.

Take the chip off your shoulder when you go for a job interview.

Inability to take criticism

There are times on the job when you may be subject to criticism (sometimes even unjustly) by your superiors or co-workers. The ability to take criticism and benefit by it is a desirable attribute. To test that ability, prior to employment, an interviewer may try to throw you off guard by some remark deliberately intended to rub you the wrong way. Don't let a discussion turn into an argument, even if you are right. It takes moral fortitude to present a point of view, but it takes diplomacy and tact to avoid an argument.

Late to the interview

"But I thought the interview was for 12:30 not 11:30." . . . "I took the wrong train." . . . "I had to wait for a cab in this rainy weather." . . . "I forgot my portfolio and halfway down here turned back home to get it." Any excuse for lateness to an interview, even a valid one, starts you off on the wrong foot. You begin the interview on the defensive.

As a safeguard against lateness, start out early enough to allow for unforeseen delays en route. If you find that you have arrived at your destination early, you can always use the spare time to good advantage. It gives you an opportunity to stop for a cup of coffee or a smoke, and to freshen up a bit. It also gives you a chance to review your résumé and your "sales pitch."

Failure to express appreciation for the interviewer's time

The good impression you make on an interviewer can be hurt if you leave the interview without acknowledging appreciation for the courtesy extended to you. If you think you did well on the interview, clinch it not merely with verbal thanks, but by following it up with a short, thank-you note. And even if you feel that you somehow failed to make a favorable impression, write a thank-you note anyway. It may help to turn the tide in your favor, especially if the correspondence includes some additional evidence of your qualifications not brought out in the interview.

Your letter may read something like this:

Dear _____ :

Thank you so much for the time spent in interviewing me for the job as Comptometer Operator. As it may be of interest to you to see the letter of commendation I spoke of, I have taken the liberty of enclosing a copy of it.

You know how very much I would like to be associated with your company and how hopefully I anticipate a chance to work for you in the near future.

Sincerely yours,

DOS AND DON'TS FOR JOB INTERVIEWS

1. Don't look annoyed if you have to wait beyond the time scheduled for your interview. Instead, keep yourself profitably occupied by reviewing your résumé or other aspects of your job presentation.

2. Don't enter the interviewer's office wearing a top coat. It's better to carry it neatly folded over your arm or leave it in the waiting room. Wearing a coat during an interview conveys the impression that you can stay only momentarily and have more pressing business elsewhere.

3. Don't begin the interview with a negative remark, such as, "It's sure stuffy in here," or, "This is certainly a difficult place to get to," or some other personal observation which may put your interviewer on the defensive. Instead, begin on the positive side, even if it is no more than a complimentary remark about the attractive décor of the waiting room or the pleasant and courteous manner of the receptionist.

4. When entering the interviewer's office, don't sit down until you are invited to do so.

5. It's a friendly gesture to shake hands, but it's best to wait for the interviewer to make the first move. It's the interviewer's prerogative to initiate this token of cordiality.

6. Don't place your portfolio, package, purse, or anything else on the interviewer's desk unless you first ask for permission to do so.

7. Try to fix the interviewer's name in your mind, and use it occasionally during the conversation. Everybody likes to hear the sound of his or her own name.

8. Put your best face forward—and that's the face with a friendly smile. A friendly smile turns strangers into friends.

9. Don't chew gum during the interview. It indicates a lack of sophistication—and also interferes with good speech.

10. Make it a point to look at the interviewer as you speak or listen. Meet him or her eye-to-eye. An evasive look bespeaks a lack of straightforwardness or excessive shyness.

11. Avoid expressions like "frankly speaking" or "to tell you the truth" or "to be perfectly honest with you." These phrases, in effect, imply that you aren't always frank or truthful.

12. Speak distinctly. Don't mumble under your breath.

13. Don't give excuses for past failures. Answer all questions honestly and show how you have actually benefited by some of your previous mistakes.

14. Be modest in your claims; let the achievements recorded in your samples or résumé speak for you. Nobody likes a braggart.

15. In presenting a portfolio as a visual part of your "sales pitch," let the interviewer set the pace in examining the contents. You must assume that the person who looks through the portfolio is quick of mind and eye and knows what to look for. If the interviewer fails to look at every one of your samples, don't say, "But you haven't seen this yet." Your samples should be clearly marked, making it unnecessary for you to keep up a running commentary.

16. "Don't smoke during an interview" is generally a good rule to follow. But if you are an inveterate smoker, and you are offered a cigarette, you may accept. Even with the interviewer's invitation to smoke, avoid lighting up one cigarette after another. Excessive smoking shows that you are tense. Don't advertise it!

17. Don't "knock" your previous employers or go into a detailed account of your gripes and grievances. There is nothing to be gained by it. Speaking against others in no way enhances your own position.

18. Don't try to ingratiate yourself by betraying confidences or revealing trade secrets of your previous employers. There is no surer way to convince the interviewer that you can't be trusted.

19. Don't listen or appear to be eavesdropping on telephone calls which may temporarily interrupt the interview. You can make discreet use of this interlude by taking note of awards, certificates or other documents or pictures proudly displayed in the office. Your observations can be the subject for some complimentary remarks when the interview resumes.

20. Remember to leave a copy of your résumé with the interviewer, even if you are not specifically requested to do so.

21. Sense when the interview is over. It's easy to tell. You'll get the cue when the interviewer rises as if ready to escort you to the door, or starts thanking you for "coming in," or begins to shuffle through some papers as if ready to resume some prior, unfinished business. Don't overstay your welcome. Leave while you're ahead!

22. Make it a point to thank the interviewer in person as well as with a follow-up note. It is advisable to forward a brief, but well-worded thank-you note for the courtesy extended to you during the interview. It also affords you the opportunity to allude to some favorable aspect of your discussion and helps to reinforce the good impression you have made.